Upper West Side Catholics

Upper West Side Catholics

Liberal Catholicism in a Conservative Archdiocese
The Church of the Ascension, New York City, 1895–2020

Thomas J. Shelley

Empire State Editions
An imprint of Fordham University Press
New York   2020   **ESE**

Fordham University Press has no responsibility for the persistence or accuracy of URLs for external or third-party Internet websites referred to in this publication and does not guarantee that any content on such websites is, or will remain, accurate or appropriate.

Fordham University Press also publishes its books in a variety of electronic formats. Some content that appears in print may not be available in electronic books.

Visit us online at www.fordhampress.com/empire-state-editions.

Library of Congress Cataloging-in-Publication Data

Names: Shelley, Thomas J., author.
Title: Upper West Side Catholics : liberal Catholicism in a conservative
    archdiocese : the Church of the Ascension, New York City, 1895–2020 /
    Thomas J. Shelley.
Other titles: Church of the Ascension, New York City, 1895–2020
Description: New York : Empire State Editions, 2020. | Includes
    bibliographical references and index.
Identifiers: LCCN 2019028505 | ISBN 9780823285419 (hardback) | ISBN
    9780823285426 (epub)
Subjects: LCSH: Church of the Ascension (New York, N.Y.)—History. | Upper
    West Side (New York, N.Y.)—Church history. | New York (N.Y.)—Church
    history.
Classification: LCC BX4603.N6 C474 2020 | DDC 282/.7471—dc23
LC record available at https://lccn.loc.gov/2019028505

Printed in the United States of America
22 21 20   5 4 3 2 1
First edition

Dedicated with gratitude to
Mrs. Elizabeth Molda (May 20, 1908–October 30, 2002)

mother of
Mrs. Irene Bogoni
A faithful parishioner of the Church of the Ascension
And an extraordinarily generous benefactor of this parish.

Contents

viii | Contents

Foreword

When I first asked Monsignor Thomas J. Shelley to write the history of Ascension Church as it comes to mark its 125th anniversary, he responded enthusiastically with a resounding "Yes." For that I am grateful, as will be many people from Ascension who will read his work.

In order to really appreciate the history of Ascension or any other New York City parish for that matter, it is necessary to know and understand the neighborhood the parish and its people and priests live in and serve in order to see and appreciate how the faith community has developed and changed over time. Monsignor Shelley has masterfully painted a colorful description of the Upper West Side and Morningside Heights as these areas changed over the decades including struggles with crime, violence, and gentrification which has tended to push out long-time (and often poorer) families. With the arrival of each group of new residents, many of whom were immigrants, beginning with Germans who were then followed by Irish, Hispanic, and now a highly diverse population, the parish adapted, sometimes not easily, to the needs of each. Shelley gives particular attention to the impact the building of rapid transit, particularly the extension of the subway lines uptown, had on the neighborhood and how this shaped the parish also.

In the early years of Ascension, the large number of parishioners were served by a pastor and four or five assistant priests. Before the 1960s, the spiritual and social needs of the people were typically served principally through more than a score of Masses each week (including more than 5,000 people coming on Sunday alone), confessionals open for many hours each Saturday, traditional devotions on weekday evenings, and myriad clubs and activities catering to the various groups in the parish (adult men and women, small children and teens). In addition, the parish school enrolled more than 900 students at its height and had both—that is, religious sisters and brothers teaching in most of the grades. For the average parishioner it was principally through all of these services and activities in both the church and school that Ascension and the wider Church touched and shaped both their spiritual and daily lives. But as much of American culture and the wider world began to change, so too was the Church affected by the changing social forces in the 1960s.

The Second Vatican Council was convened by Pope John XXIII and took place from 1962 to 1965. Many would say that the role of the Church as well as that of priests changed radically after its conclusion. But the role of the laity changed dramatically also, empowering them to play a more active part in the life and even governance of the Church—no longer being told to simply "pray, pay, and obey." Ascension Parish took the mandates of the Second Vatican Council quite seriously. As early as 1966, the parishioners of Ascension were studying its documents, especially those pertaining to the liturgy and the rights and responsibilities of the laity. Energized and empowered through their study of these documents, in 1968 when Ascension was awaiting a new pastor, a group of parishioners got together to offer their recommendations to the new archbishop, Terence Cooke, about the selection of their next pastor. While their input seemingly fell on deaf ears, their efforts to be heard demonstrated that times had certainly changed. And it was also a harbinger that more things would change, or would have to, in the years ahead.

Despite all that has changed in Ascension and in the wider communities it seeks to serve, a few core values have remained constant. The parish, its priest, and people continue to work to create a vibrant Catholic community, especially by welcoming all who are new. Each Sunday, a warm word of welcome is extended to those who may be at Ascension for the first time and to those who are visiting: regardless of the newcomer's or visitor's language or gender, sexual orientation, and marital or document status. As one woman once commented to me: "I'm so grateful to you for your welcome, because after all, the kingdom of God never excludes—it always invites! That's what the kingdom of God is all about, and I'm glad that that's what we are about here at Ascension!"

Father Daniel S. Kearney,
Pastor, Church of the Ascension
Ascension Thursday, May 30, 2019

Abbreviations

AANY   Archives of the Archdiocese of New York
ACA   Archives of the Church of the Ascension
AFSCNY Archives of the De La Salle Brothers of the Christian Schools
ASCNY   Archives of the Sisters of Charity of New York

"J'espère mourir un religieux pénitent et un libéral impénitent."
("I hope to die a penitent religious and an unrepentant liberal.")

Henri Lacordaire, O.P.

1802–1861

1

A Home of Their Own

Parade Time

Americans have always loved a parade, whether they lived in large cities or small villages. No celebration of the Fourth of July would have been complete without a parade, no matter how modest it might have been in a small town. This was especially true in the later nineteenth century when many Americans were members of veterans' organizations like the Grand Army of the Republic, labor unions, fraternal fellowships, and ethnic and religious societies. They were always eager to demonstrate their strength in numbers by participating in civic and religious events like the dedication of a new city hall or court house or church.

At that time the residents of the Upper West Side of Manhattan were no different from the rest of mainstream America. They jumped at every opportunity to take part in a parade. Therefore, on June 28, 1896, when Michael Augustine Corrigan, the archbishop of New York, presided at the blessing of the cornerstone of the new Catholic Church of the Ascension on West 107th Street, it would have been unthinkable if the festivities did not include a parade through the streets of the neighborhood. The parishioners were joined by lay members of twenty-six Catholic parish and fraternal societies from all over New York City. They added solemnity to the occasion by marching through the streets in something less than serried ranks carrying flags and banners accompanied by brass bands playing hymns and patriotic songs. They included contingents even from long-vanished organizations like the Catholic Benevolent Legion and the Society of Catholic Mechanics and Tradesmen.

In the over-the-top style of nineteenth-century journalism, the reporter for the *New York Times* pulled out all the stops and predicted sight unseen that the future church would be "one of the most magnificent on the Upper West Side." He estimated that almost 5,000 people were in attendance at the blessing of the cornerstone. Not to be outdone in hyperbole, the reporter for the *New York World* claimed that no fewer than 600 children, all clad in white, took part in the ceremonies.

Unfortunately, Mother Nature did not cooperate for the occasion. It rained cats and dogs all day, leaving the participants drenched to the skin despite a forest of umbrellas. The parade included an appreciative salute to the first two temporary homes of the parish. The assembly point was the first home of the parish, the Lion Park Hall on West 108th Street. From there the marchers proceeded down Columbus Avenue to 106th Street, then passed in front of the second home of the parish, the Home for the Aged of the Little Sisters of the Poor, before turning north on Amsterdam Avenue to 107th Street. Many buildings along the route were decorated with inter-twined American and papal flags. The pastor of the new church, Father Nicholas M. Reinhart, served as the master of ceremonies.

It is not known if anyone dared to explain to Archbishop Corrigan the vital significance of the Lion Park Hall in the origins of the parish. It was owned by the adjacent Lion Lager Bier Brewery, where many of the German-born parishioners were employed. One can only wonder about the real sentiments of one of the honorary chaplains to the archbishop, Father James Galligan, a neighboring pastor who had fought tenaciously to prevent the establishment of the new parish.

The ceremonies had a pronounced Teutonic flavor, as befitted the occasion since the new church had been established primarily for the benefit of the German-speaking Catholics in the neighborhood. The Grand Marshal was Mr. Joseph Stultzenberg, and there were two sermons, one in English by Father Joseph Campbell, S.J., the president of St. John's College (the future Fordham University), and another in German by Father Jerome Henkel, O.F.M. Cap. They spoke to a "sea of dripping umbrellas," according to one press report. After the conclusion of the ceremonies, there was a dinner and reception at the Lion Park Hall, where there was said to be "general rejoicing." It is likely that most of the rain-soaked guests were celebrating with Lion Lager Bier (the house brew) rather than with ginger ale or iced tea.[1]

The Dedication of the Church of the Ascension

By November of that year the church was almost entirely enclosed physically. It was used for the first time on Sunday, March 14, 1897, when six Masses were celebrated in the church, which was said to have ample room for 1,200 worshippers. That estimate also seems a gross exaggeration even though poor urban Americans grew shorter and slimmer in the late nineteenth century. The church was designed in the Romanesque style by the German-American architectural firm of Schickel and Ditmars.[2]

A recent succinct description captures the salient features of the building.

The blessing of the cornerstone of the Church of the Ascension, June 28, 1896. (*New York World*, June 28, 1896.)

The façade, which is faced with light-colored rough stone and limestone trim, includes a triple portal entrance surmounted by a rose window, and four small turrets. Inside, the Italianate nave has a decorated ceiling, wheel windows at the clerestory level, and tall side aisles with faux-marble columns. Above the white marble high altar is a richly colored stained glass window depicting the Ascension of Christ.[3]

The pipe organ was the work of the local firm of Müller and Abel, both German immigrants. The much-admired stained-glass window of the

The interior of the Church of the Ascension. (Photo by Seth Webster.)

The Organ and Choir Loft of the Church of the Ascension. (Photo by Seth Webster.)

Ascension of the Risen Lord behind the main altar was also a link with the Fatherland. It was manufactured in Munich and was the gift of an anonymous donor in 1897 shortly before the completion of the church. Left unsaid was that the side and rear walls were brick, not stone, for the same reason that the church was built in the middle of the block rather than on the corner of Broadway where real estate was much more expensive.

Appropriately, on Ascension Thursday of that year, May 27, 1897, Archbishop Corrigan returned to dedicate the church. Once again there was a parade from the Lion Park Hall to the church that included a large number of clergy, parishioners, church societies, and bands.[4] Father Reinhart had every reason to be proud of what he had accomplished in two years as the founding pastor of the Church of the Ascension. However, at the blessing of the cornerstone in June 1896, the enthusiastic reporter for the *New York World* had made the wild prediction that the church would be completed and the entire debt paid off by Christmas of that year. Neither prediction proved to be accurate. Archbishop Corrigan was less than pleased when the parish debt on the uncompleted church reached the sum of $133,000 by the end of 1896. He was so apprehensive that he appointed two senior pastors to investigate the finances of the parish.[5]

The Archbishop and the Pastor

The two people who deserve the most credit for the establishment of the Church of the Ascension were Michael Augustine Corrigan, archbishop of New York from 1885 until 1902, and Father Nicholas M. Reinhart, the pastor of Ascension from its founding in 1895 until his death in 1900. They were as different as chalk from cheese in age, family origins, personality, and the scope of their accomplishments. However, each of them—the aging archbishop from a comfortable middle-class family in Newark, New Jersey, and the dynamic young priest from the Lower East Side of Manhattan—made his own distinctive contribution to Ascension.

Archbishop Corrigan

Archbishop Corrigan holds the record for establishing new parishes in the archdiocese of New York, no fewer than 99 during his seventeen years as archbishop. In a pastoral letter that he issued in April 1900, he said that, during the previous decade, he had opened a new church, chapel, school, convent, rectory, or institution every two weeks, a total of over 250 buildings.[1]

Archbishop Corrigan was the *wunderkind* in the American Catholic Church in the late nineteenth century. He climbed the greasy pole of ecclesiastical preferment so rapidly that he became the bishop of Newark and the youngest bishop in the United States at the tender age of thirty-four. As coadjutor (assistant archbishop) to the ailing John Cardinal McCloskey of New York (1880–85) and as archbishop of New York (1885–1902), he was an indefatigable worker who administered his sprawling archdiocese during his first ten years without the help of a single auxiliary bishop. He also was a born bureaucrat who was more comfortable reading financial reports than interacting with people.

Politically he was intensely conservative, comfortable with Tammany Hall, and opposed to labor unions like the Knights of Labor despite the fact

Michael Augustine Corrigan, archbishop of New York, 1885–1902. (Author's personal collection.)

that Terence V. Powderly, the Grand Master Workman of the organization, and many members were Catholics. He was also suspicious of any movement or individual who could remotely be described as liberal or socialist, including Cardinal James Gibbons, the archbishop of Baltimore, the leading figure in the American hierarchy. "To speak my thoughts without reserve," he once told a priest who was helping him establish his new seminary at Dunwoodie, "I could not tolerate the liberalism attributed to His Eminence of Baltimore."[2]

Historians have not been kind to Archbishop Corrigan. "With the best intentions in the world," said John Talbot Smith, the first historian of the archdiocese of New York, "[Corrigan] caused more controversy [in New York] in a decade than the Catholic body had known in its history." Many of his difficulties with his clergy can be traced to the fact that "candor was not a virtue that he practiced with any regularity," in the suggestive words of Marvin R. O'Connell, the perceptive historian of the diocesan clergy. O'Connell added that Corrigan "displayed a weakness—not unique to him by any means—for surrounding himself with second-rate functionaries who could pose no threat to him." Even Corrigan's most sympathetic biographer, Florence D. Cohalan, commented that Corrigan's "love of indirect methods . . . infuriated his opponents and bewildered his friends." Robert Emmett Curran put it more bluntly when he observed that Corrigan "seemed unable to translate private piety into public probity."[3]

Cultural Diversity, Nineteenth-Century Style

However, there was another side to Corrigan. He also had a deep sense of his pastoral responsibility to the hundreds of thousands of Catholic immigrants, especially Germans and Italians, who were pouring into his archdiocese during his administration. His cordial relationship with German-American Catholics was unusual for a prelate of Irish ancestry in that era when Irish-American bishops were more likely to browbeat German Catholics to assimilate as quickly as possible into the American mainstream. By contrast, Corrigan vigorously defended the right of German-American Catholics to preserve their language and culture in America. "There is no harm in it," he told the members of the German Catholic Central Verein at a meeting of their organization in New York City in 1894. "If a man uses both languages, is there any sin or shame in it?" he asked.[4]

The following year he continued to practice what he preached about recognizing cultural diversity by establishing a new parish on the Upper West Side of Manhattan, the Church of the Ascension, primarily for German-speaking Catholics, although it was never exclusively a German "national parish." The origins of this new parish went back five years, to the fall of 1890, when two German-American priests appeared before the Board of Diocesan Consultors, the principal advisory body to the archbishop, and asked Archbishop Corrigan to establish this new parish. The archbishop was amenable to the proposal and said that he would ask the abbot of St.

John's Abbey in Collegeville, Minnesota, a community of German-American Benedictine monks, to take charge of the projected new parish. An indication of the archbishop's earnestness is that the following year he persuaded the abbot to send several German-speaking monks to establish St. Anselm's church in the Mott Haven area of the South Bronx, where there was a large German Catholic population.

However, over the course of the following five years, the proposal to establish a German Catholic parish in the Upper West Side stalled when it became the subject of lively discussions and opposition at many of the monthly meetings of the diocesan consultors. It was not entirely an ethnic dispute between Irish and German clergy. German pastors who stood to lose some of their parishioners to the new parish were as opposed as their Irish confrères to the establishment of the new parish.

Two of the most vocal opponents of the proposed new parish were Irish pastors of neighboring parishes, Father James Galligan of Holy Name Church, then located at West 97th Street and Bloomingdale Road (Broadway), and Father Matthew Taylor of Blessed Sacrament Church on West 71st Street. Father Taylor claimed that there were only two dozen German families in the Upper West Side. He was challenged by Father Godfrey Schilling, who said that, in fact, there were more than 250 German Catholic families.

Confronted with these contradictory claims, Archbishop Corrigan twice appointed committees to examine the situation. The second committee reported to him in January 1894 that there was definitely no need for a German church on the Upper West Side and that the German Catholics themselves were not supportive of such a parish. The next year the archbishop overruled the recommendations of the committees, took matters into his own hands, and established a new parish ten blocks north of Father Galligan's church on West 97th Street.[5]

Father Nicholas M. Reinhart

For the pastor of this new parish, the archbishop wanted a priest who was fluent in both English and German. He found him in Father Nicholas M. Reinhart, a thirty-four-year-old native New Yorker who grew up in the heavily German area of the Lower East Side of Manhattan known as *kleindeutschland* ("Little Germany"). An alumnus of St. Joseph's Provincial Seminary in Troy, New York, he was ordained in 1886. His first two assignments had been as a curate (associate pastor) in two German national parishes, Immaculate Conception on Staten Island and St. Mary Magdalen on East 17th Street in Manhattan.[6]

A Slovak Apprenticeship

Father Reinhart then had to endure a difficult apprenticeship as temporary pastor of two Slovak national parishes before he became the founding pastor of Ascension.

Archbishop Corrigan first appointed Father Reinhart the interim pastor of the Slovak national parish of St. Elizabeth of Hungary on East 4th Street. It was a challenging assignment, not only because Reinhart did not speak a word of Slovak but also because of the notorious factionalism among the Slovak laity and the rivalry between Slovak priests. Reinhart quickly discovered that there were two rival Slovak parishes within a stone's throw of one another on East 4th Street, St. Elizabeth of Hungary and the Church of St. John Nepomucene.[7]

However, Father Reinhart did so well there that, when he left St. Elizabeth of Hungary for another assignment, the parishioners interrupted their constant litany of complaints to Archbishop Corrigan to inform him without a hint of irony that "it is our pleasant duty to mention here that we have nothing whatsoever to say against our Reverend Father, the Reverend Nicholas Reinhard [sic], except his inability to understand us and our inability to understand him."[8]

In keeping with the age-old axiom that no good deed goes unpunished, Archbishop Corrigan then assigned Father Reinhart as the interim pastor of another contentious Slovak parish, the Church of the Most Holy Trinity in Yonkers, where he quickly won the confidence of the parishioners and completed the unfinished parish church that the previous pastor had threatened to sell because of a quarrel with the parishioners. A good measure of his challenge in Yonkers is that he was one of eight pastors during the first ten years of the parish.[9] However, despite his achievement of pacifying the Slovaks in Yonkers, Father Reinhart urged Archbishop Corrigan to replace him with a Slovak-speaking priest as soon as he could find a suitable candidate.[10]

First Pastor of Ascension

Archbishop Corrigan followed Father Reinhart's advice eight months later and rewarded Reinhart by appointing him the first pastor of Ascension. After walking gingerly over ethnic quicksand as an outsider in his first two interim pastorates, Father Reinhart seemed delighted to be on firmer ground with his first permanent pastorate. Fresh from his successes on East 4th Street and in Yonkers, the thirty-four-year-old Reinhart plunged into his new assignment with the boundless energy and enthusiasm of a young man

Father Nicholas M. Reinhart,
founding pastor of the Church
of the Ascension, 1895–1900. (Archives
of the Archdiocese of New York.)

who was finally the master of his own ship. However, his grasp of parish finances soon proved to be another story.

The boundaries of the new parish extended from West 101st Street to West 114th Street between the Hudson River and Central Park. When he arrived in the fall of 1895 on the Upper West Side, Father Reinhart had neither a church nor a rectory. He lived in a private residence at 228 West 104th Street, but he celebrated Mass on Sundays in a nearby banquet hall that was made available to him without charge by the owner. On the first Sunday that he celebrated Mass there, about 200 people showed up. On the second Sunday there were about 700 people. He was told by those "well acquainted people in the neighborhood" that there were 3,000 or 4,000 Catholics in the area who rarely or never attended Mass. Later he upped the figure to 7,000 people.[11]

One tidbit of information that Father Reinhart failed to mention in his voluminous correspondence with Archbishop Corrigan was that the banquet hall where he was celebrating Mass on Sunday was located on the grounds of a brewery.

The Lion Lager Bier Brewery

In the 1890s New York City was the third-largest German-speaking city in the world, after Berlin and Vienna. In virtually every German neighborhood in New York City and throughout the United States until the enforcement of Prohibition under the 18th Amendment in 1920 and the advent of modern refrigeration, there was a local brewery to provide German-Americans (and many other Americans of various ethnic backgrounds) with ample supplies of the poor person's champagne. In 1895, the year of the establishment of Ascension church, the fourth-largest brewery in the United States was George Ehret's Hell Gate Brewery, which was located a few miles east of Ascension church on the other side of Central Park.[12]

Although German immigrants were not as numerous on the Upper West Side as in Yorkville on the Upper East Side, they could boast of their own neighborhood brewery, the Lion Lager Bier Brewery, which occupied approximately six square blocks between Central Park West and Amsterdam Avenue from 107th Street to 109th Street. The site, known as Lion Park, contained not only a brewery, but also a saloon, *biergarten*, and a hall that was used for dances and social gatherings. Many of the brewery workers were Catholics from Bavaria who wished to have a church where they could attend Mass on Sunday and hear a sermon and go to confession in their native language. Since the hall at Lion Park did little business during the winter months, the proprietor (who was not a Catholic) generously allowed Father Reinhart to use it *gratis* for Mass on Sunday mornings while he was starting his new parish in November 1895.

Archbishop Corrigan might have frowned on the celebration of Mass in Lion Park, but Father Reinhart's difficulties did not stem from the strait-laced archbishop but from the vigilantes of the Anti-Saloon League, who threatened the owner of Lion Park with the loss of his license on the specious grounds that he was serving beer within 200 feet of a place of worship. The owner appealed for help to Father Reinhart, who offered a spirited reply. "I am a fighter," Father Reinhart told the press, "and I am ready to fight this issue. The manager of the brewery was doing a good work when he gave us the use of the hall, and it is outrageous that he should be criticized. It is perfectly proper for us to meet where we do and we shall continue to do so." However, in the spring of 1896 Father Reinhart moved the location of his Sunday Mass from Lion Park to the chapel of the Little Sisters of the Poor at their Home for the Aged on West 106th Street. Reinhart's motive was not fear of the Anti-Saloon League but his consideration for the plight of the owner of Lion Park, who needed his hall back for wedding receptions.[13]

Making No Small Plans

Father Reinhart made no small plans for the future of his new parish, but he soon discovered that his lager beer purse was inadequate to support his champagne taste. He envisioned a large church on a corner site that would dominate a major intersection. His first choice was the southeast corner of West 106th Street and Amsterdam Avenue, but the owner of the site demanded $100,000, which Reinhart's real estate agent described as "absurd." Another possibility was the northwest corner of West 106th Street and Amsterdam Avenue, which was available for $86,500, but even that location was too expensive.[14]

Like many a Manhattan pastor before and since, Reinhart resigned himself to the fact that he had sufficient financial resources only to build his church in the middle of the block.[15] The corner lots, he informed the archbishop in somewhat shaky English, were "not for our purpose pruden-tial to buy." He suggested three possible names for his new parish. One suggestion was absolutely bizarre (Ecce Homo) and another was embar-rassingly self-serving (St. Nicholas). The third was Mater Dolorosa. Arch-bishop Corrigan rejected all three suggestions and decided that the new Catholic church on the Upper West Side would be called the Church of the Ascension.[16]

With the approval of Archbishop Corrigan, by January 7, 1896, Reinhart purchased four lots on West 107th Street between Broadway and Amster-dam Avenue for $34,000. With admirable foresight, shortly thereafter Reinhart bought four additional adjacent lots on West 108th Street for another $36,000, for a future school.[17] It must have been music to the arch-bishop's ears when Reinhart informed him that "a [parochial] school in this vicinity is an absolute necessity." Two years earlier Corrigan, a firm believer in Catholic schools, had told a Catholic German-American audience, "No bishop in the United States ever appoints a German pastor but he feels sure that in due time a schoolhouse will be erected."[18]

As was mentioned already, Archbishop Corrigan was so shocked when the parish debt reached the sum of $133,000 in 1896 that he appointed two senior pastors to investigate the finances of the parish. Father Reinhart responded to their criticism as vigorously as he had once responded to the criticism of the Anti-Saloon League. A year later the grand total of his expen-ditures was $148,000, and he had not yet begun construction of the rectory or the parochial school he intended to start in the fall.

Rather than apologize for this lopsided balance sheet, Reinhart did not think there was any reason for him to be alarmed at the financial condition of his parish, although his debt included a mortgage of $94,000 and out-standing loans of $21,000 from banks and individual creditors at 6 percent interest. As far as Reinhart was concerned, it was all water off a duck's back. "We need not fear," the incurably optimistic Reinhart blithely assured

Archbishop Corrigan, "as the congregation is growing rapidly, and every Sunday the collections are amazing and never less than about $235."[19]

A financial analyst today might shudder at Father Reinhart's naïve optimism and urge the archbishop to remove him as pastor before the sheriff arrived on the scene to repossess the church and property. However, Archbishop Corrigan, who micromanaged the finances of every parish in his archdiocese down to the last detail, may have seen redeeming personal and pastoral qualities in Father Reinhart that compensated for his naïve fiscal optimism. Whatever the archbishop's motives may have been, he left Ascension's first pastor in charge of the parish until his untimely death of pneumonia at the age of thirty-nine on December 26, 1900.

As far as Father Reinhart is concerned, he may have been as shrewd as he was optimistic, perhaps a passive-aggressive practitioner of the venerable clerical strategy that it is easier to beg for forgiveness afterward rather than seek permission beforehand. In any event, his legacy to Ascension is the impressive church he built on West 107th Street.

3

The Upper West Side

Manhattan Moves North

Manhattan has been moving north ever since an inquisitive Dutchman (or perhaps a French-speaking Walloon) in seventeenth-century New Amsterdam stuck his head above the parapet of the wooden palisade on Wall Street and decided to explore what lay farther north.[1] The famous gridiron map of Manhattan, which obliterated many of the beautiful natural physical features of the island, dates from 1811, but decades were to pass before all of the avenues and streets on the map were actually laid out and paved, and the surrounding neighborhoods began to fill up with houses and people. By 1860 the population of New York City was larger than that of most American states, but virtually all New Yorkers resided south of 59th Street.

After the Civil War, Manhattan continued its relentless march north of 59th Street on both sides of Central Park, creating two loosely demarcated neighborhoods, the Upper East Side and the Upper West Side. The young Edith Wharton, on her return to New York City in 1872 after spending several of her childhood years in France, Italy, Spain, and Germany, was not impressed with either the East Side or the West Side of Manhattan, or, for that matter, with any area of New York City. She described it as "a cramped horizontal gridiron of a town without towers, porticoes, fountains or perspectives, hidebound in its deadly uniformity of mean ugliness." She admitted that fifty years later it was a totally different city.[2]

The Upper East Side

The Upper East Side led the way in this transformation. It was richer and more prestigious than its geographical cousin on the other side of Central Park. The Upper West Side could not boast of anything comparable to the elegant mansions erected on Fifth Avenue during the Gilded Age by some of the wealthiest robber barons in the United States before the advent of the income tax, inheritance taxes, or the living wage. Ward McAllister, the indefatigable social climber and chronicler of New York society, declared that "a fortune of a million dollars is only respectable poverty."

Herman Melville was less impressed than McAllister with New York society. "The class of wealthy people are, in aggregate," he said, "such a mob of gilded dunces that not to be wealthy carries with it a certain distinction." Collis P. Huntington, the railroad tycoon who made a fortune from the construction of the transcontinental railroad, lived on Fifth Avenue across the street from Cornelius Vanderbilt II, but even he had to agree to pay a "service fee" of $9,000 to McAllister to gain access to the charmed inner circle of the "Four Hundred" who constituted the cream of New York society.[3]

Real estate development proceeded at a much faster pace on the Upper East Side than on the Upper West Side. Then as now, real estate development in New York City was inextricably entangled in local politics, and local politics in the 1860s meant the ubiquitous presence of "Boss" William Tweed, grand sachem of Tammany Hall (the powerful local Democratic organization) and commissioner of the Department of Public Works. Tweed and his friends, the so-called Tweed Ring, made huge profits from their investments on the Upper East Side, where real estate values skyrocketed thanks to generous public works projects funded by the city. The "Tweed Ring" wanted no competition from real estate developers on the Upper West Side.[4]

The Upper West Side

A milestone in the development of the Upper West Side was the construction of the Dakota between 1882 and 1884, New York City's first luxury apartment building, located at Central Park West and 72nd Street. It was well named. Vintage photographs show the tall Victorian apartment building standing embarrassingly alone in the midst of empty lots and shanties. The opening of the Dakota sparked a fitful rash of real estate development on the Upper West Side.

Four spacious north–south avenues—Broadway, West End Avenue, Riverside Drive, and especially Central Park West—were eventually lined with mansions and upscale apartment buildings while the two other main north–south arteries, Ninth Avenue (Columbus Avenue) and Tenth Avenue (Amsterdam Avenue), never acquired the same social cachet and were flanked with residential buildings and stores that catered to a more working-class population.

The young Alfred Kazin was especially impressed with the majestic array of luxury apartment buildings that lined Central Park West in the

The Dakota apartment building, c. 1895. (Museum of the City of New York.)

early twentieth century. "And what a parade of names to those castles on CPW," he said, "the El Dorado, the San Remo, the White House, the Kenilworth, the Ardsley, the Beresford, the Dakota, the Orwell." Even the doormen over-awed him. "In their starched wing collars and white dickeys," he said, they "made me think of aged retainers in the House of Lords."[5]

The same social differentiation was evident on the side streets as on the avenues, with rows of attached townhouses, many of them classical New York brownstone row houses for the upper middle class and tenements for those of more modest means. The heyday of the New York brownstone was now over. "No chocolate brownstone uniformity here," said the historians Edwin G. Burrows and Mike Wallace, but rather individualized, eclectic, historical styles jumbling together Jacobean, French Gothic, and Dutch Renaissance. "Indeed," they said, "McKim, Mead & White touched off a Dutch Colonial revival in 1885, with their row houses on West End and 83rd."[6]

In 1880 a real estate developer told the West Side Association that the presence of some 2,500 shanties and their occupants prevented "respectable people" from settling in the neighborhood. Some of the shanties were built

West End Avenue, looking south from West 95th Street, c. 1889. (Museum of the City of New York.)

by squatters recently evicted from Central Park. A more enlightened local resident complained about the attention that the West Side Association gave to attracting "merchant princes" to build palatial residences on Central Park West and Riverside Drive while failing to consider the need to provide "good substantial houses for the accommodation of persons of moderate means who were likely to populate the side streets."[7]

When tenements were constructed on the side streets for the poor and working class, they hardly met the criteria for "good substantial houses" even by nineteenth-century standards. The priest-historian Henry Browne, who grew up in a tenement in the West Side in the 1920s, used his own personal experiences to describe what he called "the culture of the tenement" in his youth. He said that "it meant climbing as many as five flights of stairs perhaps several times a day. Sometimes it was to the roof to hang wet wash. It meant to be without steam heat, electric lights, inside plumbing, or even hot water, bath tub or shower, without refrigeration or closet space." Browne added, "While New York Catholics erected ever more impressive churches, they did not live in them."[8]

The most common type of tenements in late-nineteenth-century New York City were five-story or seven-story buildings called "dumbbell tenements" because of their shape, which consisted of two four-room apartments in the front and two three-room apartments in the rear connected by a narrow hall. The four apartments shared two toilets. The earliest version of the "dumbbell tenements" lacked even that primitive amenity. Privies were located in the basement and there was no running water above the first floor. Most of the windows looked out onto a dark airshaft less than five feet wide between adjacent buildings, and the airshafts often became foul-smelling garbage dumps and fire hazards. Elevators were an unthinkable luxury. The landlords were frequently immigrants themselves, known as "cockroach capitalists."

"Dumbbell tenements became the fetid heart of the urban environmental crisis," said the historian Allen J. Share. "In them disease and death festered and spread throughout the rest of the urban body." They were ideal breeding grounds for consumption (tuberculosis), which Archbishop John Hughes once described as the natural death of the Irish immigrant. Bad as the situation was on the Upper West Side, it was even worse in the slums of lower Manhattan. In 1890 the death rate from tuberculosis was 49 per 100,000 on the Upper West Side; in lower Manhattan it was 776 per 100,000. When the construction of these tenements was outlawed by the Tenement House Law of 1901, they housed about 2.3 million people, two-thirds of the recently enlarged city's population, and they continued to be used by thousands of the poorest New Yorkers well into the twenty-first century.[9]

The sudden enlargement of the city's population at the end of the nineteenth century was due to the establishment of Greater New York City on January 1, 1898, when Manhattan annexed the Bronx, Queens, Staten Island, and Brooklyn (the fourth-largest city in the nation). The consolidation created the largest city in the United States. "Gotham, with 3,437,202 people, had moved into another league altogether," said Mike Wallace, "one of planetary scale, in which it was outranked only by London (6,506,954 in 1901)." The municipal government issued a commemorative brochure advertising it as "Second City of the World."[10]

The Ninth Avenue El

In addition to Boss Tweed's vested interest in the Upper East Side, another reason for the sluggish growth of the Upper West Side was the lack of adequate mass transit facilities to lower Manhattan. Until 1870 there was a one-track horsecar line on Eighth Avenue (Central Park West) that ran a single car back and forth between 59th Street and 84th Street. The only alternative form of public transportation was a stagecoach that ran once an hour on the Bloomingdale Road (later renamed the Boulevard and still later renamed Broadway in 1899). In 1879 the geographer and cartographer

The Ninth Avenue El, looking south on Columbus Avenue, 1879. (Museum of the City of New York.)

Egbert L. Viele foresaw a bright future for the Upper West Side, with a preposterously extravagant prediction that gives hyperbole a bad name. Viele said that the Upper West Side would soon rival Paris, Berlin, Vienna, Rome, and "the finest portions of the West End of London." He and many others pinned their hopes on the completion of the Ninth Avenue Elevated Railway from South Ferry to the Upper West Side. That year the opening of the Ninth Avenue El to 81st Street gave the Upper West Side its first rapid transit facility, but it did not lead immediately to the building boom that it was expected to produce.

The El served a very useful purpose for the residents of the Upper West Side. The first of four elevated railways constructed in Manhattan in that era, the Ninth Avenue El eventually ran north from South Ferry to West 155th Street with a parallel branch line that ran north from South Ferry on Sixth Avenue and reconnected with the Ninth Avenue El at West 53rd Street. It provided frequent and inexpensive access to the heart of both midtown and downtown Manhattan, but it did little to improve the aesthetics on Ninth Avenue as steam engines showered ash and hot cinders on the street below and the sound of screeching brakes continued long into the night.

A character in William Dean Howells's novel *A Hazard of New Fortunes*, published in 1890, declared that the Third Avenue El was "the most ideal way of getting about in the world" although she had said shortly before that "nothing under the sun could induce her to travel on it." Another snobbish character in the novel preferred the East Side elevated lines to the West Side lines because the former attracted a poorer clientele and offered him "continual entertainment." He explained that he "never entered a car without encountering some interesting shape of shabby adversity, which was always adversity of foreign birth."[11]

On the Ninth Avenue El, safety was problematic, especially when the miniature tank locomotives and the wooden gate cars negotiated the charmingly named 90-degree "suicide curve" at the intersection of 110th Street and Eighth Avenue (Cathedral Parkway and Frederick Douglass Boulevard). The tracks ran on top of a spindly elevated structure that was the height of

A steam-powered northbound Ninth Avenue El train negotiates the "suicide curve" at 110th Street and 8th Avenue, 1894. (New-York Historical Society.)

a six-story apartment building. Some passengers claimed that, as the train rounded the curve, they could hear the angels sing. Rapid transit on the Upper West Side improved substantially with the electrification of the El in 1903. It improved even more the following year with the coming of the West Side IRT subway on Broadway and especially with the construction of the IND line on Central Park West in 1932. Having outlived its usefulness, the Ninth Avenue El was demolished in 1940.

In 1880, the year after the Ninth Avenue El reached the Upper West Side, there were still thirty-four streets between 59th Street and 125th Street that had not been completely graded and paved. That same year Riverside Drive was opened to the public, but, as the historian Charles Lockwood complained, "It still lacked the finishing touches that made a great boulevard." According to Lockwood, even the broad north–south avenues were still unpaved dirt roads, and "water and gas lines were few and far between" on the Upper West Side.[12]

Nevertheless, a mere six years later, the *New York Times* was bullish on the prospects for the Upper West Side:

> The west side of the city presents just now a scene of building activity such as was never witnessed before in that section, and which gives promise of the speedy disappearance of all the shanties in the neighborhood and the rapid population of this neglected part of New York. The huge masses of rock which formerly met the eye, usually crowned by a rickety shanty and a browsing goat, are being blasted out of existence. Streets are being graded, and thousands of carpenters are engaged in rearing substantial buildings where a year ago nothing was to be seen but market gardens or barren rocky fields.[13]

Over the next few decades, many of these predictions became a reality, especially on Morningside Heights. Construction began on the still uncompleted Cathedral of St. John the Divine at 112th Street and Amsterdam Avenue (1892); Teachers College moved uptown to new quarters on 120th Street (1894); St. Luke's Hospital relocated from Midtown to Amsterdam Avenue and 113th Street (1896); Columbia University established a massive presence on Morningside Heights with a thirty-two-acre campus on Broadway (1897); that same year Barnard College moved from Midtown to Morningside Heights and Grant's Tomb was completed on Riverside Drive; Jewish Theological Seminary followed the northward trek of other educational institutions with a new building at Broadway and 123rd Street (1902).

Last but not least, Union Theological Seminary, founded in 1836 and soon to establish a national reputation, also moved to Morningside Heights (1910). In the meantime, Morningside Park was completed from 110th Street to 123rd Street in 1895 to provide suitable greenery for the eastern façade of the city's new American acropolis.

The Broadway Behemoths

The opening of the West Side IRT subway in 1904 triggered a building boom of luxury apartment buildings on the Upper West Side that finally provided the residents of the Dakota with more presentable neighbors than the denizens of the neighborhood shanties. "After the turn of the century," said Mike Wallace, "the right address for tens of thousands of professionals, businessmen and white collar workers lay on Manhattan's [Upper] West Side." Broadway led the way with the construction of a dozen or more massive apartment buildings that Wallace dubbed the "Broadway Behemoths."

One of the earliest was the Ansonia, constructed between 73rd and 74th streets in 1904. It was a seventeen-story Parisian Belle Epoque residential hotel with a staff of 240 employees that featured 18-room apartments which rented for $625 a month. It even boasted a rudimentary form of air conditioning based on the refrigeration system used in the New York City slaughterhouses. A few years later it was eclipsed in size by the Apthorp, which claimed to be the largest apartment building in the world, and then by the Belnord, both of which occupied a whole square block surrounding a center courtyard. The parade of luxury apartment buildings continued up Broadway to Morningside Heights for more than a decade. They were complemented by the only slightly less opulent apartment buildings on the principal crosstown streets and on Central Park West and Riverside Drive. By 1912, West End Avenue had been transformed from three- and four-story buildings into "a canyon of twelve-story structures."

By far the grandest of all the new buildings that appeared on the Upper West Side was not an apartment house but a mansion erected on Riverside Drive between 73rd and 74th streets by Charles M. Schwab, the steel magnate, at a reputed cost of $7 million. It was an imitation French Renaissance chateau surrounded by a landscaped miniature park and included a private chapel and a banquet hall for 1,500 guests. Schwab chose the location perhaps not only for the view of the Hudson but also, as Mike Wallace has mischievously suggested, because Fifth Avenue was now "congested with millionaires."[14]

Ascension School shortly after its completion in 1912. (Archives of the Archdiocese of New York.)

New York: A Catholic City?

By 1860 the population of New York City had grown to 813,669 from 312,710 in 1840.[15] In 1860 one of every four New Yorkers had been born in Ireland and one of every six New Yorkers had been born in Germany. Not all of these immigrants were Catholics, but about one-third of the German immigrants were Catholics, and, after 1830, the great majority of the Irish immigrants were Catholics with the result that by the end of the Civil War Catholics may have constituted the majority of the city's population. They were certainly the largest religious community not only in New York City, but also in the state and the nation.[16]

In New York City, at least, Catholics were not only becoming more numerous, but some of them were becoming rich and generous benefactors of Catholic causes. None of them could rival the wealth of the Vanderbilts or the Rockefellers or the Morgans. When J. P. Morgan died in 1913, leaving an estate of $68,300,000, Andrew Carnegie muttered, "And to think he was not a rich man."[17] However, John Crimmins, a devout Catholic, made his fortune as a contractor, especially in the construction of the first New York City subways, and even made his way into the charmed circle of the "Four Hundred."

Eugene Kelly was a successful banker and William R. Grace was a shipping magnate. Thomas Fortune Ryan was probably the wealthiest Catholic in New York City thanks to his investments in the diamond mines in the Belgian Congo and his ownership of several New York City streetcar companies. Neither enterprise was noted for enlightened treatment of their employees. In 1892 the *New York Tribune* claimed that there were 1,103 millionaires in New York City, but scarcely more than two dozen of them appear to have been Catholics.[18]

At the other end of the social spectrum in New York City were the horse-car drivers and conductors who worked as long as sixteen hours a day without even a lunch break.[19] Many of them were Irish Catholic immigrants. When 6,000 of them went out on a strike called by the Knights of Labor in January 1889, they paralyzed the city for a week. They received little sympathy from either the largely Irish police force or the *New York Times*, which claimed that the strikers were ignorant men who were setting themselves "against the force of law and order and against civilization itself." Archbishop Corrigan was equally unsympathetic, since he regarded the Knights of Labor as a subversive secret society. One of the few prominent Catholics who came to the aid of the strikers was Archbishop Corrigan's nemesis, Dr. Edward McGlynn, the controversial priest who had recently been excommunicated by Vatican officials for his involvement in reform politics in New York City and his support of the Home Rule Movement in Ireland.[20]

One outraged observer of the strike was William Dean Howells, who gave a graphic fictional account of the strike in which he depicted one cynical policeman predicting that, after one week, the strikers would return "with their tails between their legs and plead to be taken on again." In fact, when the workers did attempt to return to work after a week, the employers refused to re-hire any striker who would not sever his ties with the Knights of Labor. "We intended to be entirely independent of all labor organizations," said one employer. One newspaper reporter said that the defeated strikers resembled "a flock of sheep going over a fence."[21]

A few Catholics became prominent in public life through their roles in municipal politics. The shameless rascal George Washington Plunkitt became the Democratic boss of Hell's Kitchen and a pillar of Sacred Heart

Church on West 51st Street. Born in 1842 on Nanny Goat Hill, an Irish shanty town in what later became Central Park, he reportedly held down three municipal jobs simultaneously while proclaiming that "the Irish was [sic] born to rule, and they're the honestest [sic] people in the world." "When Plunkitt controlled street cleaning in New York," said Richard White, "he cleaned up but the streets remained dirty."[22] A more commendable representative of Catholics in public life was William R. Grace, who was elected the first Catholic mayor of New York City in 1880 and promptly demonstrated his integrity by asserting his independence from Tammany Hall.

Two other Catholics were elected mayor before the end of the century, Hugh J. Grant in 1888 and Thomas F. Gilroy in 1892. Both were Tammany stalwarts. The emergence of Catholic political power posed a serious threat to the dominance of the ruling WASP elite. In 1871 James Raymond, the editor of the *New York Times*, warned ominously that "there is an established church and a ruling class in New York, but the church is not Protestant and the ruling class is not American."[23]

Another sign of the rising Catholic political influence in New York City occurred in 1871 when "Honest" John Kelly succeeded the ousted Boss Tweed as the head of Tammany Hall.[24] The son of Irish immigrants, Kelly was married to the niece of Archbishop John McCloskey. He had a genius for organization. It was said that "he found Tammany a horde and left it an army." The first historian of the archdiocese of New York, Father John Talbot Smith, was an eyewitness to these momentous changes. He thought that New York was a predominantly Catholic city from about 1885 until the creation of Greater New York in 1898.[25]

Even as Catholics became more noticeable in New York City in the later nineteenth century, at least among the poor and the working class, there was little institutional evidence of this increased Catholic presence on the Upper West Side. Many of the residents in the new dumbbell tenements were probably Irish or German Catholic immigrants or their children, but they had to travel a considerable distance to find a Catholic church on Sunday morning. At the end of the Civil War, there were only two Catholic churches in the sixty-six blocks between the Paulist church of St. Paul the Apostle on 59th Street and the German national parish of St. Joseph of the Holy Family on 125th Street. Over the course of the following half-century the archdiocese of New York attempted to remedy that situation with the establishment of three additional churches. One of them, of course, was the Church of the Ascension.[26]

4

The Ascension Parish Plant

On Top of the World

The Notre Dame historian Jay Dolan observed that, during the first half of the twentieth century, American Catholics felt with good reason that they were "on top of the world." The Catholic population of the United States almost doubled in those decades from 12 million in 1900 to 21 million in 1940 despite a series of restrictive immigration laws in the early 1920s. Catholics were no longer predominantly poor immigrants. Many had relatively well-paying blue collar jobs. Some were now securely ensconced in the middle class.

The heartland of American Catholicism in that era was the large industrial cities of the Northeast and the Midwest (today's Rust Belt), where the local Catholic parish church was often the most prominent institution in predominantly Catholic neighborhoods, so much so that Protestants and Jews sometimes referred to the neighborhood where they lived by the name of the nearest Catholic church. Pastors commonly referred to their "parish plant" by which they meant not only their parish church but also their school, rectory, convent, and sometimes even a parish hall and gymnasium that was the center of their parishioners' social world as well as their religious life. The parish plant often served as the nucleus of a self-contained Catholic subculture. Jay Dolan quoted Dorothy Day as saying that "Catholics were a nation apart, a people within a people, making little impression on the tremendous non-Catholic population of the country."[1]

The versatile historian and economist Charles Morris ventured the prediction that "an alien anthropologist landing in a working-class Philadelphia parish in the 1930s or 1940s would know instantly the centrality of religion in the lives of the inhabitants."[2] If this mythical anthropologist had landed on the Upper West Side of Manhattan instead of in Philadelphia in the 1940s, he would also have known instantly that he had stumbled upon a very different world from a typical American Catholic working-class neighborhood of that era. Upper West Side Catholics were different. They were as devout as those in Philadelphia, but Upper West Side Catholics did not live in an isolated Catholic enclave.

They lived in a cosmopolitan world inhabited by both rich and poor people; people of many different ethnic backgrounds and social origins; academics, businessmen, and laborers; representatives of a long-established Protestant community; a rapidly growing Jewish population, both observant and secular; and people of no religious faith at all. The White Anglo-Saxon Protestants were the first New Yorkers to discover the advantages of the Upper West Side; Irish immigrants from lower Manhattan followed them north in the 1870s; the first Jewish residents settled in the area after World War I and were followed by a wave of Jewish refugees from Nazi Germany in the 1930s with the result that they soon outnumbered the Irish population and gave the neighborhood a distinctly Jewish complexion. After World War II the influx of Hispanics, African Americans, and Asians added to the cosmopolitan nature of the area.

In 1965, after a three-year study of the area, the Harvard-trained sociologist Joseph P. Lyford concluded that the Upper West Side had one of the densest residential populations of any city in the world. He defined the Upper West Side as the 125-block area between Central Park and the Hudson River from 82nd Street to 106th Street. The total population was 152,000 (40,000 of them Jewish), more than 1,000 people per block. "Only in Honolulu," he said, "is there a greater confusion of blood, ancestry, language, and culture in so small a space."[3]

As early as the 1930s, the architectural features of each broad north–south avenue provided an instant peek into the social diversity of the neighborhood. There were stately mansions and elegant apartment buildings for the wealthy on Central Park West and on Riverside Drive, spacious upscale apartment buildings for the upper middle class on Broadway and especially on West End Avenue. If West End Avenue had been wide enough for a center island filled with flowering trees and bushes, it would have rivaled in elegance Park Avenue on the other side of town. For working-class and poor families, there were four- or five-story tenements, and boarding houses for single immigrants in converted brownstones, on Amsterdam and Columbus avenues and on the side streets. It was in these boarding houses and tenements that the bulk of the Catholic population was to be found.

The Ascension "Parish Plant"

During his brief five years as the founding pastor of Ascension parish, Father Nicholas Reinhart constructed a spacious and beautifully appointed

Monsignor Edwin M. Sweeny, pastor
of Ascension, 1901–23. (Archives
of the Archdiocese of New York.)

church that remains today as his legacy to the parish. His successor, Father
Edwin M. Sweeny, was also a native of New York City, born in 1856. He
followed the typical path to the diocesan priesthood in that era, the Jesuit
College of St. Francis Xavier on West 16th Street, followed by four years at
St. Joseph's Provincial Seminary in Troy, New York. He was ordained in
1887 and appointed the pastor of Ascension on January 14, 1901, less than
three weeks after the death of Father Reinhart.[4] Like every pastor of a big-
city parish, Father Sweeny was expected to complete Father Reinhart's work
by liquidating the debt on the church and creating a "parish plant" that
would include a parochial school and residences for the sisters and brothers
who were to provide the teaching staff.

By 1904, Ascension had 5,200 parishioners and 530 children in the
Sunday School program, taught by 83 volunteer lay teachers. During the
previous year there were 226 baptisms and 71 marriages. The valuation of
the church property was $325,000; income for the previous year was
$34,566.82, a far cry from the $325 that Father Reinhart got in the collection
on a good Sunday. Ordinary expenses amounted to $8,255.04 plus addi-
tional costs for such items as debt reduction, interest payments, and
improvements to the church and rectory, which brought the total expenses
to $29,747.99, leaving a surplus of $4,818.83. The single biggest item listed
under ordinary expenses was the salaries of the clergy (Father Sweeny and

his three assistants), which came to a hefty $2,500 compared with $315 for coal and wood, $393.01 for gas and electricity, and $51.67 for the luxury of a telephone.

In addition to the passing of the collection basket at Sunday Mass, two other archaic forms of fundraising persisted at Ascension in its early years. One was pew rent, which meant leasing a pew to a family for their exclusive use for a year. The rent was payable quarterly in advance. It did more to flaunt social status (whatever that might mean at Ascension) than to promote liturgical piety, but it was an important source of parish income. It disappeared in most New York parishes in the early twentieth century.[5]

Reliance solely on the offertory collection at Sunday Mass proved to be an inadequate substitute for the loss of the revenue from pew rental in many parishes. The decrees of the Fourth Provincial Council of New York in 1886 officially referred to the offertory collection as the "penny collection."[6] Pastors devised an ingenious way of supplementing their income by introducing the practice of collecting "seat money" at the door of the church before Mass on Sunday whether or not a parishioner could actually find a seat inside the church. As the ushers scrambled to make change from dollar bills, the scene evoked embarrassing biblical comparisons with Jesus expelling money-changers from the temple.

Pastors commonly established a sliding scale for seat money with a higher fee for the more popular later Masses on Sunday morning. At the Church of the Holy Name on West 96th Street, Father James Galligan charged five cents at 6:00 A.M., ten cents at 7:00 and 8:00 A.M., and fifteen cents at 9:00, 10:00, and 11:00 A.M. Once a year he announced from the pulpit that the fees were voluntary. He claimed that the higher fees at the later Masses discouraged indolence in his parishioners.[7]

The pastor of the Spanish Church of Our Lady of Guadalupe on West 14th Street complained in the 1920s that the ushers at the Jesuit Church of St. Francis Xavier on West 16th Street badgered poor Spanish immigrants when they were unable or unwilling to pay the ten-cent seat-money fee. At St. Michael's Church on West 34th Street, parishioners who failed to pay the seat-money fee (which was as high as twenty-five cents) were confined behind a grill in the rear of the church like steerage passengers on a transatlantic liner. The practice of collecting seat money (although not the graduated fee) persisted in many New York parish churches until the 1950s or even later.[8]

Sacramental Life
On Sunday mornings at Ascension there were "low Masses with instruction" at 6, 7, 8, 9, and 10 o'clock and "a high Mass with sermon" at 11

o'clock. No parish in New York City had a Sunday Mass later than 11 o'clock until Dr. Edward McGlynn introduced a noon Mass at his parish of St. Stephen on East 28th Street in the 1880s. It attracted 2,500 worshippers to his parish every week, many of them working people who had given up the attempt to attend Mass earlier on Sunday morning. "Churches are for the people, not the people for the churches," McGlynn informed Archbishop Corrigan. When neighboring pastors criticized McGlynn for introducing his noon Mass and called it "The Mass of the Weak," he said such accusations "come with poor grace from any who have so much leisure every day of the week and are so generously supported by our hard-working people."[9]

At Ascension, as in virtually every New York parish, on Sunday evening at 8:00 there was a service consisting of vespers, a sermon, and benediction of the Blessed Sacrament. On weekday mornings there were three Masses, at 7:00, 7:30, and 8:00. One surprising statistic was the number of people who received Holy Communion, 34,150 annually (many of them of course repeaters), a surprisingly high number at a time when Pope St. Pius X had not yet begun to reform Eucharistic piety by mandating and encouraging early and frequent reception of the sacrament.

The sacrament of penance was an integral element in the spirituality of many Catholics, and confessions were available at Ascension every Saturday afternoon and evening from 4:00 to 10:00. Many devout Catholics would not dare to receive Holy Communion without first going to confession, although there was no obligation that required them to do so unless they were conscious of being guilty of serious sin.

In contrast to the emphasis on confession, the sacrament of baptism was treated in a rather nonchalant, even slipshod, way, not only at Ascension but in every parish church. There was neither an interview with the parents beforehand nor any baptismal catechesis because neither was considered essential in a pervasive Catholic culture. A priest was available in church on Sunday afternoon from 3:30 to 6:00 for the baptism of infants. The only requirement was that the father should be present together with two Catholic godparents. Since infants were baptized within days of their birth, the mother was rarely present at the baptism.

Parishioners were assured that requests for a priest to visit the sick or dying at home would receive prompt attention, although there is a hint of irritation on the part of the clergy in the peremptory request in the parish bulletin that the arrangements should be made by "someone who can give an intelligent account of the case." The same parish bulletin urged parishioners not to wait until the last minute to summon a priest, in effect anticipating by a half-century the decision of the Catholic Church to rename the sacrament of extreme unction the sacrament of the sick.[10]

Parish societies were an important means of involving people in the spiritual and social life of any parish. Less than a decade after the establishment of Ascension, there were ten specialized societies or sodalities for men, women, boys, and girls, each with a priest moderator and regularly scheduled monthly or even weekly meetings. One of the smallest but most important societies in every parish was the St. Vincent de Paul Society, a diocesan organization whose members visited impoverished parishioners in their homes to provide them with financial assistance. The heart and soul of the St. Vincent de Paul Society in New York for many years was Mr. Thomas Mulry, the president of the Emigrant Industrial Savings Bank. In 1892 Mulry estimated that during that year the St. Vincent de Paul Society provided financial aid to families in New York City with 11,000 children, almost half of whom would otherwise have been sent to institutions.[11]

A few years later, Josephine Shaw Lowell, a devout Unitarian, the first woman Commissioner of the New York State Board of Charities, and the founder of New York City's Charity Organization Society, recommended Mulry for the new position of Commissioner of Charities of Manhattan and the Bronx. She said, "The ten thousand helpless and suffering men, women and children in our public institutions need the protection and care of a man of his character and capacity."[12]

The Ascension Parish School

Upon his arrival at Ascension in January 1901, Father Sweeny discovered that the parish already had a small, overcrowded school located at 262 West 107th Street. He planned to replace it immediately with a much larger school, but a series of illnesses (including meningitis) forced him to delay his plans. In 1905, at the cost of $12,000, Sweeny purchased real estate on West 108th Street to add to the property that Father Reinhart had bought for a school in 1896.

On May 28, 1911, Cardinal Farley (who had succeeded Archbishop Corrigan in 1902) blessed the cornerstone of the new school in a colorful ceremony that included a color guard from the Knights of Columbus, a detachment of the New York 69th Regiment, and members of many parish Holy Name societies. The band from the Mission of the Immaculate Conception on Staten Island played hymns and patriotic songs.[13]

The school was completed the following year at a cost of $120,000 and dedicated on Sunday, September 8, 1912. Classes began the next day with an enrollment of 500 children. The school was a four-story building with

West 94th Street looking west toward Hudson River, c. 1889. (Museum of the City of New York.)

an auditorium on the ground floor that could accommodate 700 people. The three upper floors contained 18 classrooms with space for 1,100 students. The walls were deliberately designed to support an additional floor for a high school at a future date. Ascension school was one of ten new Catholic schools that were opened that year, seven in Manhattan and three in the Bronx, bringing the total number of parochial schools in the archdiocese to 185 with 1,805 teachers, 1,092 of whom were sisters or brothers.[14]

For the first four years the sisters lived at Holy Cross convent on West 42nd Street, and the brothers lived at Manhattan College, which was then located at Broadway and 131st Street.[15] In 1916 Father Sweeny rounded off his parish plant with the purchase of a house for the Sisters of Charity at 302 West 106th Street at a cost of $32,000, and another residence for the Christian Brothers on West 105th Street at a cost of $15,000. All told, his expenditures for the school and the two residences came to a total of $179,000.[16]

Like Archbishop Corrigan, Cardinal Farley exercised close oversight over parish finances. The fact that Father Sweeny received permission to spend such an unusually large amount of money (most of it borrowed) over the course of a dozen years indicates Cardinal Farley's trust in Father Sweeny's financial acumen.

In the spring of 1916, Sweeny gave Farley an account of his financial management. "My gross debt will be $105,000," he told the cardinal, but he assured him that it would be "a debt very easy to handle" because his yearly Sunday collections were almost $50,000. His yearly expenses were about $16,000 for the church and rectory, about $13,000 for the school, and about $5,000 for interest on the debt, leaving a surplus of about $15,000 for payments on the debt and extraordinary expenses.[17]

The Ascension Parish House

Cardinal Farley rewarded Sweeny for his services to Ascension by making him a monsignor in 1917, a meaningful distinction before the subsequent wholesale inflation of the distribution of honorary papal honors. However, Sweeny was not yet finished with his plans for enlarging the size of his parish plant. In 1920 he discovered that a closed and derelict Protestant church at 12 West 108th Street between Central Park West and Manhattan Avenue was available for sale at $70,000.

He wanted to purchase it and transform it into a Parish House and Club. However, the interior of the building was in such poor physical condition that a real estate agent advised him that it would cost another $25,000 to renovate it. Sweeny received permission from the new archbishop, Patrick J. Hayes, to spend a total of $95,000 to purchase the building after successfully pleading that he had cut the debt in half during the previous four years and that he could liquidate the remaining debt of $43,500 during the following two years. Sweeny's extensive renovations included an extraordinary luxury, the installation of a swimming pool. One youngster noted that the pool was unheated, but he commented, "We are Irish and are used to swimming in cold water."[18]

By 1923, if not before, the Ascension Parish House could boast of a full round of social and athletic activities for the estimated 5,000 families in the parish. Management of the Parish House was in the hands of five officers and a ten-member Board of Governors, all lay people, both men and women, who were elected annually. Participation was open to any family in the parish who paid a monthly fee of fifty cents.

For adults, the Dramatic Society presented several plays a year in neighboring parish auditoriums, and the Mothers' Club sponsored frequent card games that included Bridge and the long-forgotten game of Big Euchre. There were basketball and swimming teams for both boys and girls that competed successfully in local parish leagues. The sight of Catholic schoolgirls playing basketball in abbreviated uniforms must have been something of a novelty since the *Ascension Church Bulletin* urged "more of the female sex [to] come over and root for them." Not surprisingly, boxing tournaments were limited to boys. It is not clear how long the Ascension Parish House remained in operation, but the building was later sold and is now a Southern Baptist Church.[19]

Over the years Sweeny periodically provided Cardinal Farley and later Archbishop Hayes with detailed accounts of how he managed the money that he received from his parishioners in the Sunday collection, but he gave no indication of the financial circumstances of these generous parishioners. However, on one occasion he mentioned parenthetically to the vicar general that many of his parishioners worked on the cleaning staffs of the buildings of Columbia University, but they were too poor to afford the rent in the "better class of apartments" that were being built on Morningside Heights between Broadway and the Hudson River.[20]

In 1901 Father Joseph F. Delaney, the senior curate at Holy Name Church, Ascension's immediate neighbor to the south, said that many of his parishioners "are of the very poor class; almost all the rest, with a few exceptions that are hardly more than sporadic, deserve to be spoken of as ordinary responsible working people." In the absence of additional documentary evidence, it seems reasonable to suppose that Father Delaney's socioeconomic profile of his parishioners would be equally applicable to Father Sweeny's parishioners at Ascension. If that surmise is accurate, it means that he built and financed his impressive parish plant almost entirely with the generous donations of many poor and working-class Catholics.[21]

Nemesis

One of the few setbacks that Sweeny suffered in his dealings with the archdiocese was his inability to prevent the loss of the northern part of his parish to the new parish of Notre Dame that was established on West 114th Street in 1910. In vain he used the same contradictory arguments that other pastors had used fifteen years earlier to prevent the establishment of Ascension parish. He claimed that the loss of the area north of West 110th Street to the proposed new parish would hurt him financially because he would lose so many generous parishioners, and, at the same time, he tried to persuade Archbishop Hayes that there were so few Catholics in that area that they could never support a new parish. Archbishop Hayes had probably heard the same self-serving arguments many times before from other pastors and remained unconvinced. The plans for Notre Dame went ahead as scheduled.[22]

Monsignor Sweeny suffered a stroke in the fall of 1923 and died eleven weeks later in St. Vincent's Hospital at the age of sixty-seven after twenty-two years as the pastor of Ascension Church. One of his survivors was his ninety-seven-year-old mother. He is remembered today as the pastor who paid off the debt and placed the parish on a firm financial basis, built an impressive parochial school, obtained the services of the Sisters of Charity and the De La Salle Christian Brothers to staff the school, and created an extraordinary parish social center.[23]

5

Bishop Joseph P. Donahue

The confident years at Ascension coincided approximately with the pastorate of one person, Joseph P. Donahue, who was pastor of Ascension from 1924 until his death in 1959 at the age of eighty-eight. A native New Yorker, graduate of Manhattan College, and alumnus of St. Joseph's Provincial Seminary in Troy, New York, he was ordained in 1895.

He might be best described as a typical brick-and-mortar pastor of his era, except for the fact that most of the brick-and-mortar work at Ascension had been done and paid for by his two predecessors. He inherited a parish plant that included a spacious church, large school, rectory, convent, brothers' residence, and even a parish hall and gymnasium.

His building accomplishments were relatively minor in comparison with those of Father Reinhart and Monsignor Sweeny. He renovated the church, school, and rectory and improved the living conditions of the sisters and brothers. In 1928 he opened a new convent for the sisters at 218 West 108th Street, adjacent to the school. Four years later he renovated the former convent at 302 West 106th Street and converted it into a residence for the De La Salle Christian Brothers, a religious community that was well known to him from his student days at Manhattan College.

As was customary in the Catholic clerical world during the confident years, a stream of honorary papal honors inexorably followed Donahue during his thirty-five years as pastor of Ascension as he rose from Father Donahue (1924) to Monsignor Donahue (1937) and then to a Prothonotary Apostolic (1939), a contrived Roman species of a super-monsignor that allowed him to play the role of a faux bishop several times a year by celebrating Mass in a miter and episcopal buskins.

A more serious and problematic promotion (because it involved real power) was Donahue's appointment in 1939 as the third-string vicar general to assist the notoriously reactionary Monsignor J. Francis McIntyre, who might accurately be described as "authority's answer to intellectual

Bishop Joseph P. Donahue, pastor of Ascension, 1924–59, as a monsignor in the late 1930s or early 1940s. (Archives of the Archdiocese of New York.)

curiosity." It was a role in which Donahue felt comfortable. Even more problematic and a source of wonderment, if not scandal, was the decision of Cardinal Francis Spellman in 1945 to appoint Donahue an auxiliary bishop of New York (there were already four) at the ripe old age of seventy-five, the mandatory retirement age for bishops today.

High Noon

High noon at Ascension occurred during the first two-and-a-half decades of Bishop Donahue's pastorate, although he had little to do with this achievement. The peak year seems to have been 1932, deep into the Great Depression, when the parish census listed 1,758 families (8,115 adults and 1,553 children) for a total of 9,668 parishioners. All but 70 families listed English as their native language. The once-prominent German presence in the parish was now reduced to 28 families, while Hispanic families as yet numbered a mere dozen. There was a token presence of other ethnic groups, including Italians, Poles, Hungarians, French, Belgians, and even one Asian family (they were still called "Orientals"). Ascension was proud to be an overwhelmingly Irish parish.

The sacramental statistics give the unmistakable impression of an active and deeply devout Catholic faith community. There were ten Sunday Masses (some of them at the chapel of the Little Sisters of the Poor on West 106th Street) attended by 7,000 people. Even on holy days of obligation, 4,500 people were present at the five scheduled Masses. Attendance at daily Mass was equally impressive, with a total of 300 people attending one of the four early morning Masses. If these statistics are accurate, Mass attendance at Ascension must have rivaled that of villages in rural Ireland or Québec. Whether they realized it or not, American Catholics, including the parishioners and priests of Ascension, were living off the spiritual legacy of the Immigrant Church.

In addition to Sunday and daily Mass, there were vespers, a sermon, and benediction of the Blessed Sacrament every Sunday afternoon. Throughout the year there was a variety of afternoon and evening novenas (nine days of prayer) and triduums (three days of prayer) to St. Anthony, St. Joseph, and the recently canonized St. Thérèse of Lisieux. The month of May featured daily devotions to Mary, and in June there were daily devotions to the Sacred Heart. Attendance varied from 300 to 500 at these devotional services. The Stations of the Cross on Fridays in Lent was an especially popular devotion, drawing as many as 900 people.

An encouraging sign for the future of Ascension in 1932 was that there were twice as many baptisms as funerals (302 versus 149). Marriages outside the Catholic faith ("mixed marriages") were still a rarity. At Ascension in 1932 only 22 of the 154 marriages were "mixed marriages." The priests at Ascension were assiduous in caring for the sick at Women's Hospital at West 110th Street and Amsterdam Avenue, which they visited daily. They also made an average of 28 "sick calls" every week to those who were confined to their homes. In 1932 they anointed 229 dying parishioners. Not one of them refused the offer to receive the sacrament of the sick and dying.

Prior to the Second Vatican Council, Catholics placed great emphasis on frequent reception of the sacrament of reconciliation, but the estimates of the numbers of the faithful availing themselves of this sacrament at Ascension strain credibility. The parish priests were available to hear confessions every Saturday afternoon and evening for five hours. The pastor estimated that 2,600 adults went to confession every week and 5,000 adults went to confession every month. An additional 1,100 schoolchildren were brought to church for confession *en masse* every month under the watchful eyes of the sisters and brothers.

If these statistics are to be taken at face value, it would mean that half of the parishioners went to confession every month at a time when canon law obliged them to receive the sacrament of penance only once a year if they were conscious of being guilty of serious sin. Theoretically the clergy at Ascension would probably have been able to satisfy such heavy demands on their time because, as early as the 1920s, there were four associate pastors, later increased to five, to assist the pastor.[1]

The state of the parochial school was also one indication of the flourishing nature of Ascension parish in Depression year 1932. There were 985 students with a faculty of 14 sisters and brothers. There were an additional 280 students in other Catholic schools, mainly high schools, bringing the total number of students in Catholic schools to 1,265. Another 211 Catholic students in three neighborhood public schools attended Sunday school or received religious instruction during the week at Ascension.

Parish societies remained popular, although reduced to five instead of the original ten. They boasted a combined nominal membership of 1,680, but only a third of the members were regular attendees at the monthly or weekly meetings of their society. Curiously, the best-attended meetings were those of the all-male Holy Name Society, which regularly attracted 350 men to their monthly meetings. Their motivation may have been as much social as religious (to get away from their wives and children for an evening), but it was the genius of the Holy Name Society to appeal to both motives to persuade men to come to church more often than just on Sunday. Last but not least, another indicator of the spiritual vitality of Ascension parish was the number of religious vocations it fostered. In 1932 there were eight young men studying for the priesthood and five young women in the novitiates of religious communities.[2]

The Impact of the Great Depression

Although the sacramental statistics, the robust enrollment in the parish societies, and the impressive number of vocations to the priesthood and the religious life all give a reassuring picture of the spiritual health of Ascension, other statistics give a revealing glimpse of the hardships that many poor and working-class parishioners had to endure during the Great Depression of the 1930s. In 1928 the total parish income was $281,145.65. Four years later, when Ascension recorded its peak enrollment of 1,758 families and almost 10,000 parishioners, the income was less than half that amount, $121,166.69. By 1937 it had slipped further to $99,979.82. One reason for the decline in income was that Ascension suffered the loss of 2,512 parishioners during the five years between 1932 and 1937.

However, other statistics suggest another reason for the decline in parish income. In 1932, many families who did not have the financial resources to move elsewhere were feeling the pinch of the Great Depression to such extent that more than one-third of them asked for financial assistance from the parish. The St. Vincent de Paul Society responded by distributing $13,432.50 to 635 families.[3]

The Not-So-Golden Years

The so-called golden years of Ascension occurred in the 1930s when the parish could boast of almost 10,000 parishioners (9,668 to be exact).[4] However, in any parish the statistics of weekend Mass attendance are of limited value (even when they are accurate) in assessing the real nature and character of the parish. They reveal little about the economic or social circumstances of the daily lives of the parishioners. Despite the impressive statistics on Mass attendance at Ascension in the 1930s, on closer scrutiny the golden years do not appear to have been all that golden for many of the parishioners during the Great Depression. Mention has already been made of the abrupt decline in the financial situation of the parish and the unprecedented appeal from many parishioners for assistance to meet their most basic financial needs.

Denis Sheahan, a graduate of Ascension school in 1944, put flesh and blood on the cold statistics when he recalled almost sixty years later the terrible impact of the Great Depression on the families of the Irish immigrants who were the mainstay of the parish. Some lived in "cold water flats"—tenements without heat. Unemployment was a persistent problem. "Our fathers broke their backs looking for odd jobs," he said. Their mothers took in wash and ironed clothes at home to supplement the family income and waited for their children to come home from school for lunch. "A bowl of tomato soup would be fine." The school in question was, of course, Ascension school, where sixty students were squeezed into every classroom and "the only tuition was being Catholic."

"This was a type of school where you couldn't flunk out," said Sheahan, "and you were sent there to be a good Catholic." At Ascension, as in most large urban Catholic schools, the girls were rigorously separated from the boys. "Looking back," said Sheahan, "it's as though the girls' side of the building did not exist. We knew they were there, but that's about all." In the boys' side of the school, with sixty obstreperous youngsters packed into a classroom, discipline could be prompt and severe. The boys' principal, Brother Victor, "could swing a right arm at anyone who showed disobedience. It was a good idea to play the little saint when he was around."

Sheahan also claimed that he and most of his classmates lived in such a narrowly circumscribed world that they did not know one end of the city from another. They hardly ever ventured outside the parish boundaries except to play basketball in the gymnasium of a neighboring Catholic school. "Beyond our own neighborhood, it was a foreign country." In the summer, instead of taking the subway to Coney Island for ten cents (five cents on the IRT to Times Square, another nickel on the BMT to Brooklyn), they swam in the polluted Hudson River until the police chased them away.

The end of Prohibition was a mixed blessing for many unemployed men in the parish with little education but who had found work in bars and breweries. "Those fathers who took those jobs and could stay away from alcohol were lucky," said Sheahan. "Many others who worked in that environment lived short lives." One lesson that he and his classmates learned from the Depression was the necessity to find a steady municipal job so that they could get married and raise a family. Many of them found that job in the ranks of the NYPD or the FDNY.[5]

In 1941, when Denis Sheahan was in the sixth grade, Ascension school graduated 124 boys and girls, almost all of whom appear to have been Irish, except for Jesus Ortiz, the lone graduate with a Hispanic name. Puerto Rican parents were slow to send their children to Ascension school because of their poverty. One Sister of Charity thought that many were too poor even to purchase the school uniform or to do without the free lunch program for their children in the four local public schools.[6]

The West Side Improvement

In the 1930s, one of the ugliest and filthiest areas of Ascension parish, and the whole Upper West Side, was the area between Riverside Drive and the

Undated photo of squatter's shanty in Riverside Park. (New-York Historical Society.)

Hudson River. As far back as 1913, the idealistic young Robert Moses, fresh from Yale and Oxford and eventually to become New York's controversial master builder and unrivaled power broker, envisioned the transformation of this eyesore into a beautiful riverfront park with a six-lane highway running through it. By the 1930s, however, this transformation was still only a dream.

In the words of Moses's biographer, Robert Caro, in the early 1930s, as Moses looked down at the river from the heights of Riverside Drive and West 72nd Street, what he saw before him was

> a wasteland six miles long stretching from where he stood all the way north to 181st Street. The wasteland was named Riverside Park, but the "park" was nothing but a vast low-lying mass of dirt and mud. Running through its length was the four-track bed of the New York Central. . . . Unpainted, rusting, jagged wire fences along the tracks barred the city from its waterfront.[7]

Not only did the steam locomotives of the New York Central belch cinders and huge pillars of smoke into the air, but this West Side branch of the New York Central was exclusively a freight line with long trains of fetid cattle cars loaded with livestock destined for the slaughterhouses in lower Manhattan. Before the advent of air conditioning, even on the warmest summer days, residents of the elegant apartment buildings on Riverside Drive frequently preferred to keep their windows closed rather than endure the stench emanating from the cattle cars on the railroad tracks below.

The municipal authorities also contributed to the wasteland atmosphere of Riverside Park by using it as a vast dumping ground for untreated garbage, especially at the West 79th Street and West 96th Street docks, where the Sanitation Department loaded the garbage onto scows that were towed down the Hudson and out to sea, where the refuse was dumped into the ocean. According to Robert Caro, during the Great Depression it was not uncommon to see frantic housewives scavenging through these garbage dumps for discarded food before the refuse was loaded onto the scows in the river.[8]

The first phase of Moses's beautification of Riverside Park was to cover the railroad tracks from West 72nd Street to West 125th Street beneath the slopes west of Riverside Drive, a project that he accomplished so successfully that many of the residents of the Upper West Side are not even aware of their subterranean existence. (Today the tracks are used by Amtrak.) Then Moses filled the park with walking paths and benches, trees and shrubs, and tennis courts and playing fields. When Moses completed his West Side Improvement on October 12, 1937, he borrowed a yacht so that he could appreciate the full sweep of his accomplishments from the middle of the Hudson River.[9]

It is a mystery how Moses financed this mammoth urban renewal project in such a short period of time. He claimed that the cost was only $24 million, a ridiculously low figure that invites comparison with the unbelievably low costs claimed by Baron Haussmann for the rebuilding of Paris during the Second Empire. Fortunately for Moses, he was spared the savage invective of the French politician who called Haussmann's bogus financial statements the *Comptes Fantastiques d'Haussmann*, a clever and untranslatable parody of the popular contemporary Paris opera the *Contes Fantastiques d'Hoffmann*.

In Moses's case, retribution came later. Caro speculates that the real cost of the West Side Improvement (including the elevated highway south of 72nd Street) was somewhere between $180,000,000 and $218,000,000. The Hoover Dam, completed in 1936 and the tallest dam in the world at that time, cost *only* a piddling $76,000,000. By 1937, no fewer than 7,000 laborers were adding the finishing touches to Riverside Park. It remains an intriguing but unanswerable question how many of them were fathers of Ascension schoolchildren like Denis Sheahan "who broke their backs looking for odd jobs."[10]

Robert Caro also notes that Moses lavished money on the area of Riverside Park south of 125th Street, but he spent relatively little on park facilities in the area between 125th Street and 155th Street, which was the area most likely to be frequented by African Americans from neighboring Harlem. An avid fan of cars and parkways (although he never possessed a driver's license), Moses built the six-lane Henry Hudson Parkway at the river's edge, isolating Upper West Siders from the Hudson River as effectively as the New York Central Railroad had done for the previous eighty years. Caro says regretfully that Moses had "the choice of giving the city's precious Hudson waterfront to either cars or people. And he had chosen to give it to the cars."[11]

6

A Parish in Transition

The Resilient Status Quo

As was mentioned in Chapter 5, the total number of parishioners at Ascension declined from 9,668 in 1932 to 7,156 in 1937 (5,777 adults and 1,388 children). All but 315 of them claimed English as their native language. In the first parish census after World War II (1945), there was a modest increase in the number of parishioners to 8,618, due largely to the increased number of children (2,070) as a result of the postwar baby boom. The parish census of that year was the first to record a sizeable Spanish-speaking population (100 adults and 150 children). Three years later there were 55 Hispanic families (all but five of them Puerto Rican) with 165 children.

Sunday Mass attendance at Ascension remained steady at 7,000, although the rounded-off figure raises suspicions that the clergy may simply have repeated the same statistics year after year. Other sacramental statistics are more reliable because they were based on written records rather than informal head counts by ushers at Mass. Baptisms averaged 300 per year, weddings 150, and funerals 175. Parish societies and devotional services like novenas remained popular, as did attendance at Ascension School which enrolled a record 1,780 students in 1945, although the enrollment dropped to 1,003 four years later. In 1949 six young men from the parish were in seminaries, and five young women had joined religious communities, almost as many as twenty years earlier.[1]

Armageddon: The 1960s

The 1960s were the most tumultuous decade in recent American history. The decade began on an optimistic note with the election of a young and charismatic president, John F. Kennedy, whose election was a source of special pride for American Catholics. It was a decade that also witnessed the election of Pope John XXIII, whose short pontificate ushered in a new age in the history of the Catholic Church. In the United States, the decade soon turned sour with the assassinations of President Kennedy, his brother

Senator Robert F. Kennedy, and Dr. Martin Luther King Jr. Throughout the decade violent opposition to American involvement in the Vietnam War abroad and die-hard resistance to the civil rights movement at home polarized American society.

No segment of American society remained untouched by the upheavals of the 1960s, not even an obscure Catholic parish on the Upper West Side of Manhattan. At Ascension the first inkling of the impact of the 1960s on the parish appeared in 1961, when the parish priests estimated that only 7,500 of the 17,500 Catholics in the parish were practicing Catholics. Nevertheless, there were still reasons for optimism. Sunday Mass attendance remained strong, with 5,500 people attending 11 Masses. Even more encouraging was the fact that there were 890 baptisms in 1960–1961, thanks to the large increase in the Hispanic presence in the parish.

The Hispanic presence was also reflected in the two largest parish societies, the Holy Name Society for men and the Sodality of the Blessed Virgin Mary for women. Both societies now had both English and Spanish sections. Two parish missions (several weeks of around-the-clock rousing evangelistic preaching) were organized that year. The English-language mission drew 1,400 while the Spanish-language mission drew 375. Still another sign of life was the enrollment at Ascension school of 728 students and a faculty of nine Sisters of Charity and five Christian Brothers as well as six lay teachers. Less reassuring was the fact that for the first time there were more children in the parish's catechetical program for public school children than in Ascension school.[2]

By the end of the 1960s, the once-thriving Church of the Ascension had declined to the point that it was only a shell of its former self. A door-to-door census in 1971 revealed that only 10 percent of the Catholics in the parish were regular churchgoers (2,400 practicing Catholics in a parish of 22,000 self-identified Catholics). Sunday Mass attendance slipped to 1,800 adults and 600 children, hardly enough to fill the church at any of the six Sunday Masses and the one Saturday evening Mass. The once-flourishing parish societies could muster only 170 members to attend their meetings, while tri-weekly Marian devotions attracted barely a hundred especially pious parishioners. There were 306 baptisms in 1971 and 80 marriages, but half of the marriages were "convalidations" (ecclesiastical rectifications) of canonically invalid civil marriages.

Religious education was an especially worrisome issue because of the implications for the future. There were 565 children in Ascension school taught by six sisters, two brothers and nine lay people, but there were many empty seats in the classrooms and enrollment was only a third of what it had been 25 years earlier. By contrast, there were an estimated 4,200 Catholic students from the parish in public elementary and high schools. Four hundred of them attended weekly religious instruction at Ascension, but only 170 came to Sunday Mass.[3]

By 1968, more than two-thirds of the 631 students were now Hispanic; 110 were Caucasian; 90 were African American; and about two dozen were Asian. Two years earlier a visitation team of the Christian Brothers reported that they were very impressed with the "good manners, politeness, respectfulness and grooming of the boys." The one area of weakness, they thought, was the poor diction of the students, which they attributed to the fact that English was a second language for many of them. Denis Sheahan would have been pleased to know that the boys and girls were now grouped "heterogeneously," in the arcane educational jargon of that day. In plain English, it meant that, with few exceptions, Ascension was now a school where boys and girls sat side-by-side in the same classrooms.[4]

The Departure of the Brothers and the Sisters

Within the space of two years, between 1973 and 1974, both the De La Salle Christian Brothers and the Sisters of Charity withdrew from Ascension school. In the case of both communities the reason was the same: the rapid decline in their numbers and the scarcity of new vocations to the religious life. Less than a decade earlier, in 1967, two years after the end of the Second Vatican Council, religious communities of both men and women were flourishing in the United States, and they were the backbone of the Catholic school system.

In the aftermath of the Council, however, they suffered a precipitous decline for reasons that have yet to be explained satisfactorily. However, the statistics are crystal clear. In 1967, there were 7,314 sisters teaching in the Catholic schools of the archdiocese of New York and the diocese of Brooklyn (4,130 sisters in New York and 3,184 sisters in Brooklyn). In 2017 only 79 sisters were still teaching in the Catholic schools of those two dioceses (36 in New York and 43 in Brooklyn). In fact there were only 3,332 teaching sisters and 643 teaching brothers in the entire United States.[5]

The Christian Brothers left Ascension first, in 1973, when their local community at Ascension had been depleted to only two brothers, and they found it increasingly difficult to maintain any semblance of community life. They were also hard-pressed to provide teachers for their many other schools in New York state.

During the sixty-three years during which the Sisters of Charity staffed the girls' department of Ascension school, no fewer than 117 Sisters of

Charity taught in the school. The overwhelming majority of them were women of Irish ancestry. When the Sisters of Charity regretfully informed the pastor of Ascension, Monsignor James Wilson, in the spring of 1974 that their community was withdrawing from Ascension school, they were not looking for greener pastures. They explained that they were working in twenty-three inner-city schools. As a result of the decline in vocations, they no longer had sufficient personnel to staff adequately all of these schools.[6]

A Muted Anniversary

Seventy-five years after the establishment of this new Upper West Side parish, it was obvious that the salad days of Ascension as a thriving Irish American parish were over, and that the reasons transcended the changes in the ethnic composition of the parish. They reflected the deeper fundamental changes that were taking place throughout the country as Catholics tried to cope with the political and social upheavals in American society, especially with the nebulous but undeniable phenomenon of "secularization," which one Irish Jesuit theologian recently described as the sense that "God is missing but is not missed."[7] However one defines secularization, it left many young Catholics indifferent to or even totally alienated from their faith. For the first time in American history, prominent public figures, attempting to describe their conflicted relationship with the Church, felt comfortable identifying themselves as "raised Catholic" or more provocatively as "retired Catholics."

American Catholics also had to come to terms with the winds of change unleashed by Vatican II, which intensified divisions between conservative and liberal Catholics. The encyclical of Pope Paul VI in 1968, *Humanae Vitae*, reasserting traditional Catholic teaching on birth control, added fuel to the fire. It was meant to reaffirm papal authority, but it boomeranged by leading many faithful American Catholics to call into question the credibility of numerous aspects of Catholic teaching on sexual morality. Reflecting on *Humanae Vitae* almost a half-century later, Peter Steinfels, former editor of *Commonweal* and former senior religion editor of the *New York Times*, as well as a faithful Upper West Side Catholic, said that the encyclical is "probably fated to go the way of Pius IX's indiscriminate denunciation of 'progress, liberalism and modern civilization'—and with similar cost to the faith."[8]

Ascension met these challenges as successfully as most American parishes. However, it seems appropriate to keep in mind the often-quoted comment of Thomas P. "Tip" O'Neill, Massachusetts Congressman and Speaker of the House of Representatives, that "all politics is local." Likewise, it might be said that the rise and fall of parishes are often due especially to local circumstances. That was certainly true of Ascension parish in the years following the celebration of its seventy-fifth anniversary in 1970.

The main cause of the decline of the parish was a local phenomenon, a violent crime wave, fueled by drugs, that affected every individual and institution in the Upper West Side and transformed it from a peaceful and attractive community into one of the most dangerous neighborhoods in Manhattan for the better part of three decades.

The Great Puerto Rican Migration

The story of Ascension parish from the late 1960s to the early 1990s is largely the story of how Ascension survived this calamity by welcoming into its parish community large numbers of Puerto Ricans and later Dominicans, who transformed Ascension from an aging Irish parish into a vibrantly bilingual Hispanic and Anglo parish. In subsequent years Ascension was to transform itself even further into an exceptionally inclusive Catholic parish that recovered the original meaning of the word "Catholic."

The Hispanic presence in New York City grew at a relatively modest pace in New York City before World War II. A major reason was the slow increase in the Puerto Rican population. Technically and legally the Puerto Ricans were not immigrants but citizens of the United States, a status they had enjoyed since 1917. However, as the sociologist Ana María Díaz-Stevens, who was herself part of the Great Puerto Rican Migration, has pointed out, "New York society, including the Catholic Church, treated Puerto Ricans more or less as if they had been European immigrants."[9]

In 1910 there were fewer than 10,000 Puerto Rico–born residents of New York City. As late as 1940 the Puerto Rican population of New York City was only 61,463, less than 1 percent of the entire population of the city. Most of them had come to the United States on a weekly steamship from San Juan, and they created two Puerto Rican neighborhoods (*barrios* and *colonias*) in Manhattan, the largest of which was El Barrio in East Harlem.

After World War II, the trickle of Puerto Rican migration to the mainland United States became a flood, in what has been described as the first airborne migration in the history of the world. The first commercial flights from Puerto Rico to the United States began in 1946. Since the planes from San Juan landed at Idlewild Airport in Queens (today's JFK airport), New York City quickly became the epicenter of the Puerto Rican migration to North America.

The Puerto Rican newcomers found employment in poorly paid jobs in factories, hotels, restaurants, and commercial laundries. Later the more fortunate men obtained better-paying jobs in the merchant marine and the Postal Service. A few were even able to establish their own small businesses. Women often found employment as domestics or worked in the still-booming New York City garment industries, where they replaced Jewish or Italian immigrants who were moving on to better-paying jobs.[10]

Like generations of Irish, Italian, and Jewish immigrants before them, the Puerto Rican migrants had to contend with low wages, deplorable housing and sanitary conditions, inadequate health care, and the bigotry of the immigrants who had preceded them to the land of opportunity. Sizing up his situation in New York City in 1947, one Puerto Rican migrant told a newspaper reporter, "I came to New York because the food situation was very bad in Puerto Rico." He added, "I don't like it here, but I hate it there. Here at least I can live."[11]

By 1950 the Puerto Rican population of New York City had more than tripled to 187,420, and it tripled again within one decade to 612,574 in 1960. By 1970 there were 817,712 Puerto Ricans in New York City, one-tenth of the population of the city, and their numbers peaked at an all-time high of 896,743 in 1990.[12] Thereafter the Puerto Rican population of New York City declined as migration from Puerto Rico subsided, job opportunities decreased, and the more prosperous Puerto Ricans in New York City moved to the suburbs. Although the Puerto Ricans remained the largest segment of the Hispanic population of New York City, the Puerto Rican population of New York City decreased by 12.8 percent between 1990 and 2000 from 896,763 to 789,172 and continued to decline thereafter.[13]

The Hispanic Apostolate

The Great Puerto Rican Migration presented the Archdiocese of New York with its greatest pastoral challenge since the massive Italian immigration of the late nineteenth century. The archbishop of New York, Cardinal Francis Spellman, responded creatively and effectively to this challenge in a way that was probably the most impressive pastoral achievement of his twenty-eight years as archbishop, from 1939 to 1967.

He sought and accepted good advice, used it to formulate an effective pastoral strategy, and selected competent people to implement it. An eyewitness, Monsignor Robert L. Stern, gave credit especially to four people in shaping Spellman's original outreach to the Puerto Rican community. Like President Abraham Lincoln's famous Civil War cabinet of a "team of rivals," who were determined to win the war despite their own personal antipathies, these four individuals were united by a common desire to provide pastoral care for the Puerto Ricans that transcended their own deep ideological differences.

Monsignor John J. Maguire, chancellor of the archdiocese, apprised Cardinal Spellman of the situation; Father George A. Kelly, a young priest sociologist, documented the gravity of the crisis with a remarkably accurate scientific survey which estimated that the Puerto Rican population of the archdiocese would reach 880,000 by 1960; Father Joseph P. Fitzpatrick, S.J., professor of sociology at Fordham University, reinforced Kelly's conclusions with the results of his own extensive research. Father Fitzpatrick, an innately modest man, delighted in the fact that he was the only person named Fitzpatrick who was ever named "Puerto Rican Man of the Year" by a grateful New York Puerto Rican community.

Last but not least, Father Ivan D. Illich, a brilliant and charismatic young priest from Yugoslavia who had recently been accepted into the archdiocese, quickly became a trusted confidant of Cardinal Spellman in shaping his approach to the Puerto Rican community.[14] Illich was a bundle of energy and an incorrigible gadfly, who delighted in tossing off such *bon mots* as: "The Catholic Church needs fewer clerics and more priests." Father Fitzpatrick never ceased to marvel at the way that Illich won and retained the confidence of the deeply conservative Cardinal Spellman, although tellingly Spellman never gave Illich a major administrative position in his own archdiocese and preferred to keep him at a safe distance far away in Puerto Rico.[15]

On the advice of Monsignor Maguire, on March 24, 1953, Spellman established a new archdiocesan office, the Coordinator of Spanish Catholic Action in the Archdiocese of New York, under the direction of Monsignor Joseph F. Connolly. Connolly's responsibility was to supervise the church's pastoral efforts on behalf of Hispanic Catholics in New York. As long as Spellman was archbishop, the office worked well (despite the clumsy bureaucratic nomenclature) because it had a clear focus and unified direction, but it was less effective under his successor, Cardinal Terence Cooke, who resisted efforts to broaden the role of Puerto Rican priests and laity in the functioning of the organization.[16]

Spellman remained deeply committed to providing for the spiritual needs of these newcomers to his archdiocese, and he was proud of what he was doing for them. In 1957 he told the Apostolic Delegate to the United States, Archbishop Amleto Cicognani, that the population of Manhattan was now one-third Puerto Rican. "I do not know whether this information is important to the Holy See," he added coyly, "but it is certainly significant to us."[17] Professor Ana María Díaz-Stevens gave Spellman high marks for his direction of the Puerto Rican apostolate. "[His] great contribution to the Puerto Ricans," she said, "was to recognize the need for the archdiocese to adopt a missionary character to the apostolate."[18]

A New Kind of New York Diocesan Priest

Spellman's most important and lasting contribution to the Hispanic Catholic community in his archdiocese was a decision that received little public attention at the time but has had enduring effects to the present day. Influenced perhaps by Father George Kelly's prediction that the archdiocese of New York would soon need 1,500 Spanish-speaking priests and perhaps also by the promptings of Monsignor John Maguire, Father Joseph Fitzpatrick, and Father Ivan Illich, Spellman realized that he could no longer leave the outreach to the growing Puerto Rican community in the hands of a few religious orders with their limited personnel resources.[19]

Instead he decided that his own diocesan priests would have to assume the major responsibility of responding to this daunting pastoral challenge. In 1953, 1954, and 1955, Spellman sent two newly ordained diocesan priests to Puerto Rico for a year to learn Spanish. He also sent six seminarians to Puerto Rico during the summers of those years. In 1956 he increased his commitment to this program when he assigned one-half of the ordination class at St. Joseph's Seminary, Dunwoodie, to Georgetown University for an intensive two-month Spanish-language immersion course.

He repeated the experiment the next year, but this time the newly ordained priests were sent to study the Spanish language and culture at what came to be called the Institute of Intercultural Relations at the Catholic University of Puerto Rico. For the next decade this institute served as the principal training school for New York diocesan priests as well as for many men and women religious who were engaged in the Hispanic ministry in New York. In April 1955 Monsignor Connolly was able to report, "New York now has more Spanish-speaking clergy, very many of them native New Yorkers, than the diocese of Ponce in Puerto Rico. There are now seventy-two parishes in New York with at least one Spanish-speaking priest."[20]

The direction of the Hispanic Apostolate remained firmly in the hands of the diocesan clergy. All three of Monsignor Connolly's successors as coordinators—James Wilson, Robert Fox, and Robert Stern—were Dunwoodie alumni and fluent Spanish speakers. And hovering over the whole operation as the vice-rector of the Catholic University of Puerto Rico was the inscrutable and indefatigable Monsignor Ivan Illich.

However, by the early 1970s, the future of the Hispanic Apostolate under Cardinal Cooke did not appear to be as promising as Monsignor Connolly had anticipated that it would be seventeen years earlier under Cardinal Spellman. To be sure, in 1972 one-quarter of the 407 parishes in the archdiocese provided services in Spanish thanks to the presence of 134 diocesan priests, 88 religious-order priests, and 74 foreign-born priests, but there were only 39 Spanish-speaking pastors and not a single Spanish-speaking cleric in the upper echelons of the administration of the archdiocese.[21]

In a rapidly changing archdiocese with diminishing financial resources, Cardinal Cooke deserves credit for his commitment to assure the continuation of parochial schools in inner-city neighborhoods, a decision that benefited many Hispanic and African American children. However, he shied away from addressing the more fundamental question of the scope and thrust of the Hispanic Apostolate. When forced to choose, however, between an emphasis on issues of social justice or pastoral activity, Cooke almost invariably came down on the side of the latter perhaps because he thought that the two choices were complementary.

Whatever Cooke's motivations, Father Robert Stern, the coordinator of the Hispanic Apostolate in the early 1970s, found to his chagrin that he was confronted with a constantly diminishing budget and an increasingly depleted staff as well as stiff opposition to his desire to introduce more lay Puerto Rican involvement into the Hispanic Apostolate. He interpreted these developments as indications that he had lost Cooke's confidence and resigned in February 1973. Stern was subsequently appointed director of the prestigious Catholic Near East Welfare Association, which he directed successfully for more than two decades. He may have found his years of service in Cardinal Cooke's chancery office a valuable apprenticeship for his involvement in the opaque ecclesiastical and secular politics of the Middle East.[22]

The Hispanic Apostolate first came to Ascension parish in an official way with the arrival of Father William J. Delaney, a young native of the Irish community in the South Bronx. Ordained in 1954, Father Delaney was the first Spanish-speaking diocesan priest assigned to Ascension. His name appears in the *Official Catholic Directory* for the first time in 1956. The pastor, auxiliary Bishop Joseph P. Donahue, the vicar general of the archdiocese, was born in 1870, eighteen years before Puerto Rico became a U.S. possession. At the time of Father Delaney's arrival in the parish, Bishop Donahue had been the pastor of Ascension for thirty-two years. He resolutely refused to acknowledge the growing Puerto Rican population in the parish and stifled every effort of the more sympathetic and pastorally minded assistant priests to reach out to the Puerto Ricans and welcome them to the parish. Father Delaney was gone within a year. Bishop Donahue remained as pastor of Ascension until his death in 1959 at the age of eighty-eight.

7

Quo Vadis?

Vatican II and Ascension Parish

The Second Vatican Council (1962–65) was arguably the single most important event in the history of the Catholic Church in the twentieth century. It
came as a bolt out of the blue to many Catholics when Pope John XXIII
announced his intention to convene the Council. The unexpected impact
of the Council has been compared to major surgery performed without
anesthesia upon a patient who was unaware that he was ill.

For example, Alan Ehrenhalt described Chicago Catholics on the eve of
the Council as largely content with the status quo in the largest archdiocese
in the United States.

> The church at the parish level in the Chicago of the 1950s was no dinosaur
> limping dejectedly toward its appointment with Vatican II. It was a thriving,
> self-confident institution, at the peak of its influence. It was not searching
> for a new identity. It was simply not very interested in change. It cared
> about tradition and authority.[1]

Ehrenhalt based his conclusions largely on his extensive research in one
working-class Southwest Side Chicago parish, St. Nicholas of Tolentine.

The progressive brand of Catholicism that flourished in Chicago during
that era under Cardinal Samuel Stritch was often contrasted favorably with
the stodgy and conservative brand of Catholicism that characterized New
York Catholicism under Cardinal Francis Spellman. In a surprising reversal
of roles, however, for at least one brief shining moment, Catholics in one
Upper West Side parish seemed more eager to embrace the liberal winds of
change wafting through the Church from Vatican II than Southwest Side
Catholics 789 miles away.

In the fall of 1966, a year after the conclusion of Vatican II, the priests
of the newly reorganized Mission Band of the Archdiocese of New York gave
a modernized version of the traditional parish mission at Ascension that

was attended by some 250 people. The focus of this week-long mission was not the traditional emphasis on sin and repentance leading to long lines at the confessionals, but the themes and documents of the Council. It included a questionnaire asking parishioners if they were interested in further study of the Council's documents, especially those pertaining to the liturgy and the role of the laity in the governance of the Church. The positive response to this innovative version of a parish mission led to the formation of a study group of about 55 people, including priests, brothers and sisters, who continued to meet in the parish convent for four months.

Energized by Vatican II, this study group attempted to carry lay participation in the governance of Ascension a step further in February 1967 when they formed a study group called "Christianity-Ascension." The occasion for the formation of this new study group, which might be described more accurately as a search committee, was the anticipated retirement of the pastor, Monsignor James A. Quinn. As was customary in such situations, the chancery office sent a perfunctory questionnaire to Ascension requesting information about the state of the parish and the qualifications to be desired in the new pastor. Many parish priests paid little attention to such questionnaires because they believed, rightly or wrongly, that they usually wound up unread in a file cabinet in the basement of the chancery office.

However, the Ascension search committee decided to take the bull by the horns and produce a bona fide assessment of the parish and its needs. It was a bold decision that would have been unthinkable prior to Vatican II. It would have been unthinkable in many traditional New York parishes even after Vatican II, but Upper West Side Catholics were different. To many of them, it seemed a reasonable and appropriate response to the request for more information from headquarters. The Ascension search committee assured the archbishop that they represented a cross-section of every racial, ethnic, and social element in the parish. They identified themselves as

Whites, Negroes, Puerto Ricans, Irish, Italians, Dominicans, etc., social workers, laborers, housewives, nurses, teachers, community organizers, lawyers, psychologists, economists, sociologists, theologians, liturgists, musicians.

They promised to offer their new pastor the help of their services, but they also warned Archbishop Cooke that it would be "disastrous" if the new pastor were to ignore the role of the laity in the governance of the parish. In a covering letter to the archbishop, they complained about the lack of leadership and missed opportunities in the parish. "We have the spiritual and material resources of a loyal laity," they assured Archbishop Cooke, but they also told him pointedly that Ascension needed leadership "dedicated to matching our unmet needs with our untapped resources."

Their final report, which was submitted to Archbishop Cooke in July of the following year, was signed by thirty-one lay people, as well as by three Sisters of Charity, two Christian Brothers, and two associate pastors, Father James Welby and Father Donald Poulin.[2]

A Parish Profile in 1968

The Ascension search committee began its parish profile with a summary evaluation of the housing in the neighborhood. "As one goes from West to East," they said, "one passes from the extremes of affluence, to middle class, to the extreme of dire poverty." As specific examples of sub-standard housing, they pointed to the notorious SROs (single room occupancies) located in "welfare hotels" between West End Avenue and Broadway, the run-down tenements between Amsterdam Avenue and Manhattan Avenue, and the poorly maintained brownstones between Manhattan Avenue and Central Park West.[3]

Urban renewal was also a prime concern for these Ascension parishioners. They believed that most of the housing in the parish east of Broadway was a prime target for demolition within a year, with dire consequences for many low-income residents who would be forced out of their homes. "We cannot allow ourselves to be practically 'urban-renewed' out of existence," they said. Still another concern was the constantly expanding footprint of Columbia University in the neighborhood in its quest for additional housing for faculty, students, and the "affluent who like to breathe the air of cap and gown." Unless the new pastor exerted strong leadership, they feared, Ascension might become the front lawn of Columbia University.

The diligent Ascension researchers were interested in not only the quality of the housing stock but also in the quality of life of the people who lived in these houses. Writing only three years after the publication of Joseph Lyford's revealing study of the Upper West Side, they confirmed how accurate and relevant his findings were with regard to Ascension parish. As evidence they cited the increased incidence of drug abuse, robbery, theft, mugging, an alarming drop-out rate among high school students, and an increase in the number of the hardcore unemployed.

The 1960 federal census reported a population of 56,000 on the Upper West Side between 100th and 110th streets. From this statistic the Ascension study group extrapolated a population of about 50,000 living within the boundaries of Ascension parish: 20,000 English-speaking, 20,000

Spanish-speaking, and 10,000 African Americans. From this statistic they further estimated that the Catholics (mainly Irish, Hispanics, and Haitians) probably constituted between 50 percent and 60 percent of the population.

It was no surprise that the majority of the Catholics were to be found among the lower middle class and the poor. That had been true at that time for almost a century. What was surprising, however, was that there was now a fair sprinkling of well-educated Catholics who were professional and business people. There were also hundreds of elderly people living in the parish. Class differences were never more noticeable than on weekends when Riverside Drive, West End Avenue, and Central Park West fell silent as the affluent and upper middle class summoned their cars from their garages and left for their country homes, while Amsterdam and Columbus avenues were alive with the sounds of poor people and their children celebrating outdoor on the sidewalks.

Parish Life

Ascension's researchers estimated that there were between 25,000 and 30,000 Catholics living within the parish boundaries, but only about 10 percent of them, 3,500, attended Sunday Mass. Like many American Catholics, these stalwart Ascension parishioners were disappointed at the limited impact that the liturgical reforms of Vatican II had, at least initially, on parish life. They were especially perplexed that the introduction of a vernacular liturgy had failed to increase Mass attendance or attract many lapsed Catholics back to the practice of the faith. However, at Ascension there was a significant difference between the reaction of English-speaking and Spanish-speaking parishioners to the new liturgy. Few people attended the sung Mass in English, but an enthusiastic overflow crowd filled the basement church to capacity every Sunday for the Spanish Mass.

The committee was somewhat disturbed that the number of people who received Holy Communion at Mass was constantly increasing while the number who went to confession was rapidly diminishing. They debated among themselves whether this change was a positive or a negative development, which was an indication of the deep attachment of many of these liberal Upper West Side Catholics to the traditional practices of the faith in which they had been raised.

Catholic education was also a major priority for the members of the committee. They were especially concerned about the absence of adequate religious education for the Catholic children in the public schools. "It seems fair to say that the public school children are second-class citizens of the parish," they concluded. As they also noted, the problem was not confined to Ascension but was widespread throughout the archdiocese. In Ascension as in many other parishes, it was a problem that was easier to identify than to solve.

Communication and Leadership

For the committee, the two biggest issues facing Ascension parish were communication and leadership: the lack of communication between the clergy and the laity, and the failure of the clergy (i.e., the pastor) to provide guidance and direction for the future in collaboration with the laity.

The search committee expressed deep appreciation to their outgoing pastor, Monsignor James Quinn, for a number of reasons. A deeply conservative man, he had served as an associate pastor under Bishop Donahue from 1926 to 1942. Unlike Donahue, however, Quinn did not wallow in

Monsignor James A. Quinn, pastor of Ascension, 1959–68. (Archives of the Archdiocese of New York.)

nostalgia for a return to the so-called good old days. The search committee credited him with bringing a new spirit to Ascension by recognizing the changing demographics of the parish, approving many of the initiatives that Bishop Donahue had rejected and especially by reaching out to the growing Hispanic population.

Aside from Monsignor Quinn, however, the search committee offered a scathing indictment of the state of the Catholic Church on the Upper West Side in 1968. They said,

> It has long enough been immobilized and pastors have been chiefly to blame. Consider any pastor from Holy Trinity to Ascension. Through old age, sickness or lack of knowledge, not a single one offers leadership or the inspiration to tackle the problems we presently face on the [Upper] West Side.

The search committee set a very high bar for the person whom they would like as the next pastor of Ascension. They wanted someone who would be sympathetic to the varied cultures of the neighborhood, possess a knowledge of community affairs, be well versed in the educational needs of a parochial school in an increasingly diversified community, have the ability to relate to university students, demonstrate by his actions that he was "a spiritual man," show evidence of parochial experience, accept a limitation of three years on his service as pastor, and be willing to be evaluated by his associates, parishioners, and the diocesan authorities. Perhaps as an oversight, they failed to mention the desirability of his being able to walk on water.

Few priests were likely to apply for the pastorate of Ascension parish under such demanding conditions, but the search committee thought they had found the ideal candidate for the job. They respectfully submitted to Archbishop Cooke as their choice Father Henry J. Browne. If the search committee's analysis of the state of Ascension parish did not set off alarm bells in the chancery office, their choice for their next pastor may have precipitated several cases of apoplexy. The chancellor of the archdiocese, Monsignor Joseph O'Brien, who was a worthy successor to Monsignor J. Francis McIntyre as a heavy-handed enforcer for the archbishop, dashed off a copy of the search committee's report to the vicar general, Archbishop John Maguire, with the annotation, "Note the recommendation on the last page!"[4]

Maverick New York Diocesan Priests

Henry J. Browne had a good claim to be considered the leading clerical maverick of his day in a conservative archdiocese that had occasionally

Father Thomas Farrell, pastor of St. Joseph's Church, Greenwich Village, 1857–80.

produced liberal priests who balked at running with the herd. Mention has already been made of the formidable Dr. McGlynn, whose mentor had been Father Thomas Farrell, pastor of St. Joseph's Church in Greenwich Village from 1857 to 1880. Farrell was that rarest of rare birds, an outspoken Irish-born abolitionist who provided the seed money for the Church of St. Benedict the Moor, originally located on Bleecker Street in Greenwich Village, the first African American Catholic church north of the Mason–Dixon line.[5] After the Civil War, Farrell's advocacy of the civil rights of black Americans in the Jim Crow South led the bishop of Richmond to denounce him to the archbishop of New York for his "extravagance about the negro" and his promotion of *negrophily* (literally, "love of black people") as if it were a sin or a crime instead of a virtue.[6]

Father Farrell's liberalism was not limited to the American scene. Seven years after Pope Pius IX condemned the existence of religious liberty in Catholic countries in his *Syllabus of Errors*, Farrell publicly expressed the hope that "all men throughout the world may soon enjoy civil and religious liberty and equality before the law."[7]

Farrell's contribution to a future *aggiornamento* was to organize a study group called the "Accademia" for like-minded priests who met on a regular basis in his rectory, where they engaged in critical free-wheeling discussions of such controversial topics as biblical inerrancy, papal infallibility, vernacular liturgy, auricular confession, priestly celibacy, and the temporal power of the pope. When the Italian government seized Rome in September 1870, bringing to an end more than a millennium of papal rule, Farrell publicly hailed the event, which led to his temporary suspension as pastor of St. Joseph's Church.[8]

Edward McGlynn's numerous conflicts with Archbishop Corrigan came to a head during the mayoral election of 1886, when he campaigned for the reform candidate Henry George despite Corrigan's order not to become involved in politics. As a result, the Holy See excommunicated McGlynn in 1887, and he remained in ecclesiastical limbo for the following five years. Despite his excommunication, McGlynn remained a popular figure among many working-class New York Catholics, and Corrigan's inability to address the McGlynn affair became a national scandal for the U.S. bishops.

Once again, in 1892, the Holy See intervened, this time to lift McGlynn's excommunication and reconcile him to the Catholic Church. Corrigan learned the news from the secular press, and he was devastated. He told his friend and mentor Bishop Bernard McQuaid of Rochester, "We are in a reign of terror" and added that "the better classes" were especially upset at McGlynn's rehabilitation. Richard Croker, the leader of Tammany Hall, who was threatened by McGlynn's popularity with the Irish working class, told Corrigan that it was "the greatest blow that the Church in this country had ever received."[9]

Late in 1894, Corrigan reluctantly appointed McGlynn pastor of St. Mary's Church in Newburgh. By that time, most of McGlynn's clerical friends had also been exiled to country parishes, leading many New York priests to observe that "the brains of the diocese is up the Hudson." McGlynn died on January 5, 1900, and was buried in Calvary cemetery. Diocesan officials refused permission for McGlynn's friends to erect a statue at his gravesite. The large bronze statue stands today in nonsectarian Woodlawn Cemetery.[10]

Dr. Edward McGlynn, pastor of St. Stephen's Church, East
28th Street, 1866–87.

Father Henry J. Browne

Henry Browne was a New York priest in the tradition of Father Farrell and
Dr. McGlynn. As a young priest with a doctorate in church history, Browne
had been appointed to the faculty of the Catholic University of America, but
he was dismissed and recalled to New York by Cardinal Spellman because
of his failure to complete a sufficiently hagiographical biography of Archbishop John Hughes. Back in New York, Browne was relegated by Spellman
to teaching history to high school seminarians.

However, the New York chancery office made a tactical mistake in its
efforts to punish Browne when it assigned him to reside in the rectory of
the Church of St. Gregory the Great on West 90th Street. The son of Irish
immigrants who grew up in a cramped "old law" tenement on West 35th

Street in St. Michael's parish, Browne was no stranger to the social problems and vibrant political culture of the West Side. Once established in St. Gregory's Church, he quickly emerged as a significant figure in Upper West Side liberal politics, especially because of his expertise in the complicated and politically charged issue of urban renewal.

The special object of Browne's wrath was arrogant bureaucrats who concocted grandiose plans for urban renewal without bothering to consult the residents of the neighborhood about their real needs. In a televised testimony before a U.S. Senate committee investigating the urban crisis in 1966, he said, "We need to listen to the poor themselves." With typical bluster, he added, for good measure, that failure to do so is "like contemplating one's navel and expecting to come up with a diagnosis of your appendix."[11]

Under Browne's leadership, the Strycker's Bay Neighborhood Council waged a long and tenacious battle to prevent urban renewal on the Upper West Side from becoming another instance of gentrification in New York City at the expense of the original low-income and middle-income residents of the neighborhood. One musically talented member of the Strycker's Bay Neighborhood Council, Flavia Alaya, gave voice to their concern in a witty parody of "East Side, West Side."

East Side, West Side,
All around the Town
Urban Renewal's upon us,
The buildings are coming down.
The new ones are luxurious,
So to hell with Mamie O'Rourke.
She can be relocated
To the outskirts of New York.[12]

Father Browne was a gifted and articulate priest who readily embraced the biblical injunction not to hide one's light under a bushel basket. At St. Gregory's he once described himself as "the resident priest-professor-community leader." For many years he not only served as the elected president of the Strycker's Bay Neighborhood Council but also claimed to have recovered the colonial name of the area from his historical researches. Endowed with sharp tongue and a strong streak of the innate Irish rebel, he was a perfect ally and foil for the most radical Jewish activists on the Upper West Side. If he had written an autobiography detailing his accomplishments, he might have been tempted to call it *Alone on the Upper West Side.*[13]

It is fascinating to speculate how long the unconventional and rambunctious but resourceful Father Henry Browne would have lasted as pastor of Ascension under pressure from both the scrutiny of demanding lay leaders on the left and the surveillance of the chancery office on the right, where he was regarded with a suspicion bordering on paranoia. In any event, he never had the opportunity to demonstrate his mettle.

In the course of 1968, the process of selecting Ascension's first post–Vatican II pastor went forward steadily but not as the search committee had anticipated. On March 8, auxiliary bishop Terence J. Cooke was appointed the new archbishop of New York. He was installed in St. Patrick's Cathedral on April 4, the same day as the assassination of Dr. Martin Luther King Jr., which touched off violent protests throughout the country. On July 19, the Ascension search committee submitted its fourteen-page report to Cooke. On September 14, he appointed Monsignor Richard B. Curtin the new pastor of Ascension.

His appointment was really a slap in the face to the now-disbanded Ascension search committee and an embarrassment to Curtin, who, through no fault of his own, possessed few of the professional or pastoral qualifications that parishioners of Ascension had hoped to find in their new pastor. It was also a harbinger of Cooke's reluctance to involve the laity in any meaningful way in the governance of the archdiocese.

A master of the soft answer that turns away wrath but concedes nothing, the new archbishop had already given evidence, in his homily at his installation the previous April, of the direction in which he intended to lead his archdiocese. "Let us improve the institutions and structures that have served us so well," he said, "making them glow with a rekindled spirit of love. Let us avoid that iconoclasm which would wear down the past before moving ahead in the present to build a future."[14]

Monsignor Richard B. Curtin

Monsignor Curtin was a native of Ascension who grew up on West 107th Street and was a graduate of Ascension school. Ordained in 1942, Curtin was an energetic, articulate, and sometimes charming individual, and a professionally trained musician who taught music at the diocesan seminary for twenty years (1946–66), but his language expertise was in Latin, not Spanish. The Ascension parish to which he returned in 1968 was vastly different from the parish that he had left in 1942. His previous assignment was as pastor of St. Peter's Church, Rosendale, in rural Ulster County. In many respects he was a fish out of water and seems to have realized that early in his pastorate at Ascension. Eighteen months after his arrival, he

Monsignor Richard Curtin, pastor of Ascension, 1968–70. (Archives of the Archdiocese of New York.)

accepted a new assignment as pastor of St. Anthony's Church, in suburban Yonkers.

Another factor in Curtin's decision to leave Ascension may have been the deteriorating financial condition of the parish. Ascension had never been an affluent parish, but it had been sustained over the years by the modest contributions of many poor and working-class parishioners. As their numbers began to decline drastically, so did the income of the parish. A total of 841 individuals or families contributed $3,394.25 to the Christmas collection of 1969. Only five individuals or families gave $100 or more, but 783 gave $10 or less (and 180 of them gave one dollar or less). The parish deficit for that year was $41,565.85, largely as a result of the subsidy from the parish to the school to make up for the school deficit of $116,596.14. The overwhelming number of names of the contributors were Irish, but there were over 100 Hispanic names and a sprinkling of German, French, Italian, and Polish names.[15]

Monsignor James J. Wilson

Monsignor Curtin's successor as pastor of Ascension was Monsignor James J. Wilson, his seminary classmate, but their pastoral experience before coming to Ascension was vastly different. Monsignor Wilson served as an army chaplain in the Philippines after World War II and remained in that country for an additional seven years, acquiring a knowledge of Spanish. Upon his return to the United States in 1952, he spent nineteen years as a curate in three inner-city parishes—St. Athanasius and St. Augustine in the Bronx, and St. Teresa's on the Lower East Side. Appointed pastor of Ascension in 1970, he served two six-year terms before retiring in 1982. Between 1957 and 1963 he had also served as the coordinator of Spanish Catholic Action in the archdiocese.

In that role, said Monsignor Robert Stern, who later served the archdiocese in the same capacity, Monsignor Wilson "achieved a real consolidation and expansion of the archdiocese's commitment to Puerto Ricans and other Hispanic Americans." Stern also noticed another characteristic about Wilson that he found especially commendable. As a result of his years in the Philippines, Stern thought that Wilson had acquired "a missionary perspective" that served him well in his relationship with Hispanic Catholics in New York.[16]

It is hard to imagine any New York priest better qualified to become pastor of Ascension in 1970 than Monsignor Wilson. Two years after Wilson's appointment to Ascension, the pastorate of Holy Name Church fell vacant. One of the associate pastors at Holy Name, Father Patrick V. McNamara, begged the chancery office not to send to Holy Name a troglodyte who "would live in a sweet reverie of faded glory."[17] It is unlikely that any parishioner at Ascension ever made that complaint about Father Wilson, but his initial years at Ascension were not all moonlight and roses for other reasons.

In the fall of 1971 a group of Hispanic parishioners formed *El Comité de Cristianos pro Justicia* and leveled criticism at Wilson for his alleged lack of concern for the Hispanic community at Ascension. Their complaints included issues large and small, such as Wilson's reluctance to employ more priests from Spain and the failure to provide a bilingual parish bulletin or missalettes.

Another complaint they expressed, the location of the Spanish-language Sunday liturgy in the basement church at Ascension, was more complicated than it appears at first sight, and the situation was not due to insensitivity on the part of Monsignor Wilson or his predecessors. There was deep division within the local Hispanic community about the proper site for the Spanish-language liturgy. While some Hispanic parishioners wanted the Mass to be celebrated in the upper church, an older group of Hispanic parishioners preferred to keep it in the lower church because they had come to regard it as "their church." When Monsignor Curtin abruptly moved the Spanish Mass to the upper church, he apparently received so many protests from members of the Hispanic community that he reversed his decision and reinstated the Spanish Mass in the lower church.[18]

Wilson fought back vigorously against the accusations from *El Comité* and accused them of unfair criticism. "Although I am not conscious of any fault," he replied graciously in Spanish, "in the interest of peace, good will and for the solution of problems that require a unified effort, I ask pardon for the offenses that I have been accused of by people who believe themselves capable of judging me, and I am confident that these people will prove capable of pardoning me."[19]

Wilson seemed especially annoyed at the accusation that he was prejudiced against bringing priests from Spain to New York. He defended himself by saying that he was not opposed to welcoming Spanish priests to New York, but he thought that they should be more carefully vetted. He explained that he had encountered instances of priests from Spain who failed to show proper respect for Hispanic Catholics in New York because they were not natives of Spain (*desprecian a los hispanos que no son de España*). By contrast, he said that there were many *sacerdotes norteamericanos* who could minister more effectively to a Hispanic congregation in New York than many priests from Spain because they had immersed themselves thoroughly in the local Hispanic culture. As an example, Wilson cited "el Padre Welby," who had spent seven years as an associate pastor at Ascension under Monsignor Quinn and Monsignor Curtin.

Wilson may not have considered himself a typical Upper West Side liberal Catholic or even have approved the use of the term, but he was not a reactionary longing for the return of the pre–Vatican II *ancien régime* in the Church. Musing about the future of parish life in New York, he envisioned a situation that few pastors (or bishops) of his day would have dared to entertain. "In view of the world-wide shortage of priests," he said, "it is possible that the parishes of the future will have only one priest, probably an elderly one, several deacons (married and celibate) and several well-trained lay leaders." He appealed to the Hispanic community to encourage more vocations to the priesthood and religious life.[20]

Privately, Wilson told the vicar general, Monsignor James Mahoney, that the committee which had criticized him consisted of only a handful of people, but he warned the vicar general that such a situation could occur in any parish. Regarding the situation in Ascension, Wilson wondered if some of the student priests from Spain who had lived in the rectory had played a role in his recent difficulties. In any event, he thought the crisis was over.[21]

Monsignor Wilson was overly optimistic. The controversy dragged on for another year, spoiling his introduction to Ascension and even leading to the temporary suspension of the parish council that he had founded in October 1970 with an admirably mixed membership of English- and Spanish-speaking parishioners. Monsignor Stern, a former associate pastor at Ascension and at that time coordinator of the Spanish-Speaking Aposto-late, was asked to intervene because he enjoyed the confidence of both sides in the dispute. He described it as a "misunderstanding and dispute between a very excellent priest, Monsignor Wilson, and so many good people in the parish." He knew many of them personally.

The initial travails of Monsignor Wilson at Ascension must have been especially disappointing and frustrating to him because of his outstanding record of working successfully with Hispanic parishioners for two decades in three different parishes. However, to place his initial difficulties at Ascension in a wider context, one might recall the comment of Dom Cuthbert Butler, the nineteenth-century English church historian, who once remarked, "[F]or better or for worse, church history is in great measure made up of the differences and quarrels of good men."[22]

Bishop Edward Head, auxiliary bishop of New York and episcopal vicar of Manhattan, helped to solve one of these "differences and quarrels of good *people*" at Ascension in the fall of 1972, paving the way for the successful pastorate of Monsignor Wilson.[23] An indication that Wilson quickly won the confidence of his parishioners at Ascension becomes evident given his turning a deficit of $41,565.85 into a modest surplus of $7,125.54 within three years.[24] He also won the confidence of Cardinal Cooke, who appointed him the first episcopal vicar of the newly established vicariate of the Upper West Side.

The Waning of the Green

One of the complaints voiced by *El Comité* was that the *Ascension Church Bulletin* was an exclusively English-language publication except for the Mass schedule and parish regulations. It was a justified complaint. The *Ascension Church Bulletin* reflected the nostalgia of many of the older Irish parishioners for the rapidly vanishing world of the Hibernian Upper West

Side. One of the major social events at Ascension every year, faithfully reported in the *Ascension Church Bulletin*, was Irish Night, always scheduled to coincide with St. Patrick's Day in March.

The most prominent parishioner of Ascension in the 1960s was Judge James J. Comerford, who lived directly across the street from the church and was also one of the leading figures in New York City's Irish American community. For nineteen years (1965–84), Comerford served as the chair of the prestigious St. Patrick's Day Parade Committee, which he ran with the self-assurance of a Prussian field marshal. In his later years, according to Calvin Trillin, "he was capable of dealing with some trifling objection from the floor [of the parade committee] with a direct order, 'Sit down and shut up. The people did not come to hear you talk.'"[25]

Ethnic insensitivity at Ascension may have reached a tipping point for many Hispanic parishioners when the *Ascension Church Bulletin* published brief articles on the history of each of the thirty-two counties in Ireland and added a new column called *Beatha in Eirinn*, "News from Ireland." There was no comparable column about news from San Juan or Santo Domingo, although Father James Flanagan, a newly ordained assistant pastor at Ascension, contributed an article (in English) about his recent visit to the Dominican Republic. He described the natural beauty of the island and the friendliness of the people, but he also called attention to the oppressive poverty that so many of the people were forced to endure.[26]

For decades the *Ascension Church Bulletin* featured numerous seasonal advertisements for hotels in the Irish Alps (a.k.a. the Catskills) located in popular summer resorts like East Durham and South Cairo. The names of these establishments left no doubt about the clientele they were seeking to attract. They included Duffy's Green Isle, The O'Neill House, Shamrock House, Griffin's Irish House, Emerald Isle House, and many others. Shamrock House featured Irish-American music every evening, and The O'Neill House provided free transportation to church without the need for anyone to specify the denomination of the church.

Another favorite summer resort for working-class Irish Americans was Rockaway Beach. A number of Irish bars in Manhattan operated summer branches of their establishments in Rockaway. One of them was the Log Cabin Grill at West 103rd Street and Columbus Avenue, which advertised that buses left from the door of Log Cabin Grill to a hotel and restaurant of the same name in Rockaway every weekend. Potential patrons were assured that "good home cooked meals were available at low prices." In 1934 the round-trip bus fare was fifty cents.[27]

By the 1970s, local Hispanic merchants and storekeepers in Ascension parish were beginning to break the Irish monopoly in the advertising pages of the *Ascension Church Bulletin* and giving readers a more accurate picture of the ethnic diversity of the parish. Duffy's Green Isle now had to share space with bilingual or exclusively Spanish-language advertisements from the Farmacia San Juan, Rudy Castilla Photo Studios, La Estrellita Shoe Store, La Mia Groceries, and the Candelaria Meat Market, which announced proudly that *"Estamos Para Servirle al Publico Hispano de este Barriada."* All of these stores and businesses were located on Amsterdam or Columbus avenues within walking distance of one another and Ascension Church.

Funeral homes had long used church bulletins as an inexpensive way to promote their services. The McGonnell family had two flourishing funeral homes in the Upper West Side, one at 175th Street and St. Nicholas Avenue and another at the corner of 107th Street and Amsterdam Avenue. The latter funeral home had long been a favorite with Ascension parishioners because of its proximity to the church. By the early 1970s, however, McGonnell's funeral home in Washington Heights had competition from an upstart establishment two blocks away, the Rivera Funeral Home, which trumped McGonnell by offering to provide transportation of the remains of deceased relatives by air to Puerto Rico and all Latin American countries.

Walter B. Cooke, Inc., was one of the largest funeral homes in Manhattan but was slow to catch on to the changing ethnic demographics of the Upper West Side. The firm placed an advertisement in the *Ascension Church Bulletin* in August 1972 announcing that "Spanish-speaking personnel [were] available at all times" at their funeral home on West 72nd Street. Unfortunately for Walter B. Cooke, Inc., the advertisement was published only in English, not in Spanish.

Ascension was not the only Upper West Side parish to experience the shockwaves of the transition from an Irish to a Hispanic parish. In his own inimitable way Father Henry Browne described the ethnic transition at the Church of St. Gregory the Great where he had been a priest-in-residence for a number of years and pastor from 1968 to 1970:

> St. Gregory's survived the leaner years of the Depression, New Deal and World War II still an "Irish parish," and until 1949 was under the regime of Monsignor Patrick O'Donnell, whose tribal connections brought several Irish societies to celebrate their Masses in the church. But by the 1950s their bagpipes in the street on Easter Sunday morning were awakening a block full of mystified Puerto Ricans, who had inherited from some of their

escaping Irish predecessors most of the tenement apartments facing and flanking the church on West 90th Street.

"The parish took some time to respond to this change," added Father Browne without further comment. Except for the bagpipes on Easter Sunday, the same could be said of the Church of the Ascension.[28]

8

A Neighborhood in Peril

Upper Broadway and the Human Comedy

In the 1970s, as the Upper West Side was experiencing a major demographic upheaval, Alfred Kazin, the literary critic, who lived on West End Avenue in the West 80s, quickly discovered that Broadway, one block from his apartment building, was an ideal vantage point from which to observe the human comedy in the neighborhood. He found that the ever-shifting population who occupied the benches on the traffic islands in the center of Broadway were especially intriguing. He noticed that

> very old-looking women who cannot be as old as they look and who are hideously made up, sit tensely and somehow angrily taking in a little sunshine. They are frequently impeded in this by drunks drooling and sprawling over them as they sip from bottles decorously contained in paper bags; by junkies who are reeling but determined to make conversation; by the transvestites, wearing falsies and pink curlers, who have neglected to shave. There is also a pair of identical sandwich men [walking billboards] who duplicate each other's knife-like nose, knobby chin and eyes. Although they do not wear disguises of any kind, they look like masked thieves about to pounce.

According to Kazin's observation, a former professor of Russian at the City University of New York sits all day on one of the benches deploring the proliferation of drunks who change places sitting next to him. A street evangelist proclaims that the King James Bible is the only version acceptable to God but occasionally interrupts his diatribe to shout at long-haired men and boys, "Be a man! Get a haircut!" A well-known neighborhood figure, the "Mad Woman of Broadway," walks into Zabar's delicatessen wearing house slippers, notices the well-dressed yuppies on line at the lox counter, and shouts at them in a heavy Yiddish accent, "Bestids, all of you." She is later seen in a drugstore talking on a telephone marked "out of order."

On West End Avenue the atmosphere was more genteel but equally interesting and unpredictable. Returning from a weekend in the Hamptons on one occasion, Kazin was surprised to find a demonstration in front of his apartment building. A dozen young black women were parading up and down on the sidewalk, denouncing a resident of the building as a slumlord because he had inherited from his father two tenements in Brownsville, one of the most poverty-stricken areas of Brooklyn. A young Jewish man with a bullhorn "who looked like pictures of Trotsky in 1905" led the demonstrators, chanting, "Ostrofsky is a slumlord! Ostrofsky is a slumlord!" Ostrofsky was a young Jewish songwriter who had recently published a scholarly book on American Calvinist theology. Such was the range of diversity as it was once practiced on the Upper West Side.[1]

To the present day, public transportation offers revealing insights into the *sangfroid* and idiosyncrasies of Upper West Side New Yorkers. A young man boards a crowded 86th Street crosstown bus at Central Park West wearing a sweatshirt that says "Property of Alcatraz Prison: Outpatient Psychiatric Department." No one rushes for the exit or even bats an eyelash.

A woman of a certain age becomes exasperated with the snail's pace of the notoriously pokey 72nd Street crosstown bus on the 66th Street transverse road through Central Park. She demands to be let off in the middle of the park. The bus driver replies that she cannot do so legally. The woman retreats to the rear of the bus and begins to scream at the top of her voice, "Emergency! Emergency! I am sick and going to throw up all over the bus." Passengers crouch low in their seats and cover their heads. The bus driver seems familiar with the routine. She stops and allows her unruly passenger to exit the bus. The woman walks the rest of the way at a brisk pace and reaches Fifth Avenue ahead of the bus.

"An Ever-Present Sense of Everyday Menace"

When the Harvard-trained sociologist Joseph P. Lyford moved to the Upper West Side in 1962 to begin his research on the area, he purchased a four-story brownstone on West 92nd Street between Central Park West and Columbus Avenue. A week later he discovered what his new neighbors meant by "airmail." It was their habit of tossing garbage and empty beer bottles into his back yard from the rear windows of the tenements that faced the back of his brownstone. When Lyford's appeals to the police and sanitation workers proved fruitless, he took matters into his own hands and cleaned the back yard himself twice a week wearing his old World War II helmet for protection from projectiles. Urban renewal forced Lyford to relocate farther north two years later to West 105th Street, a few blocks east and south of the Church of the Ascension.[2]

His new neighborhood was only marginally better than his old neighborhood on West 92nd Street. He said that West 105th Street "seemed to be more or less an internment camp for welfare mothers and large numbers of children who went to Sunday school, jumped rope, and sometimes turned in false alarms." Despite such snide remarks, all too reminiscent of President Ronald Reagan's disparaging reference to "welfare queens," Lyford recognized that the women were the most stabilizing element in the community. He admired especially the efforts of mothers to shield their children "from the world of the pusher and the hoodlum." Speaking more like a psychologist than a sociologist, Lyford said that, in this environment, "fear and protectiveness were the signs of healthy resistance, like fever. If the fever subsided," he explained, "it meant that the family had broken apart, with the children spinning off in all directions."

Lyford's harsh comment about the prevalence of "welfare mothers" in his new neighborhood is belied by his own observation that most of the people who used the IRT subway station at Broadway and 103rd Street to go to work and come home from work many hours later were women. He estimated that about 20 percent of the men on his block were unemployed. The situation was even worse a block away on West 104th Street, where he thought that at least half of the male population was out of work and would never find jobs. "They were beyond the reach of any poverty program," he said. "Many of them should have been in mental institutions for their own protection as well as for the safety of others."[3]

A few years later, in 1969, a reporter for the *New York Times* confirmed Lyford's observations about living conditions for many people in the West 100s. He found that the sub-standard housing was especially difficult for Hispanics and African Americans, who lived in rundown brownstones, rooming houses, and deteriorating residential hotels between 100th and 110th Streets. One Hispanic resident told him, "Five years ago this neighborhood was not too good, but not too bad. Now it is terrible." She said this standing before the grimy façade and broken front door of her apartment building on West 103rd Street.[4]

During his brief sojourn on the Upper West Side, Joseph Lyford came to share many of the views of his newly acquired friend Father Henry Browne, especially Browne's critical view of local politicians and bureaucrats. Browne was an historian and Lyford was a sociologist, but Lyford was impressed with Browne's insightful and witty spoof of the New York City government when he compared it to the Empire State Building "without elevators." "Somewhere up on top," Browne said, not altogether tongue-in-cheek, "is the administrative apparatus, the public is in the basement, and in between is a vast air space occupied by the civil service."

The consequence of this three-tiered arrangement, Lyford argued, is that "the unaffiliated citizen lives in nearly total bewilderment about his government, and, on their side, the administrative officials work in general ignorance of what their own bureaucrats are doing to the citizen." A half-century later many New Yorkers would find this analysis a prophetic description of their relationship to their municipal and state government today.[5]

One colorful and sometimes carnival-like feature of Upper West Side society in those days was the ubiquitous presence of a plethora of "community organizations" that ranged from the St. Gregory's Mothers' Club to the Young Assassins. Lyford thought that many of them had no active membership except a handful of people who regularly elected each other as officers and sent off resolutions to the *West Side News*.[6]

Father Browne demurred. He loved these community organizations. The more controversial and obscure they were, the more they appealed to his populist instincts. On more than one occasion, he hosted meetings of three or four organizations on the same evening in St. Gregory's rectory. They included such diverse groups as the United Farm Workers, La Mia Buying Club, Friends of Welfare Rights, Hudson River Sloop Conservation Group, Straphangers United, and Many Races Cultural Foundation.

Apparently the Young Assassins did not make the cut. However, Father Browne allowed the Gay Liberation Front and *Venceremos*, a pro-Castro Cuban group, to meet at St. Gregory's provided that they did not advertise their meeting. *Venceremos* canceled their scheduled meeting because of a conflict in dates. "It was probably better," said Browne, "than risking that the pious anti-Castro parishioners might have begun another revolution." Their opinion of Browne has not been recorded.

On the evening of April 21, 1970, Father Browne was about to serve as the master of ceremonies at a rock concert honoring Father Philip Berrigan, a Josephite priest, who was one the most prominent anti-war activists of the day. Berrigan had jumped bail and was hiding in the rectory. As the ceremonies were about to get under way, the FBI broke into the rectory and arrested him. The rock concert took place without him. As Browne related the incident in melodramatic fashion, a hundred armed, trench-coated FBI agents were crouching in the doorways of adjacent buildings, surrounding the church and waiting in vain for the arrival of Berrigan's more elusive Jesuit brother, Daniel, an equally prominent anti-war activist.[7] A further embellishment of the incident identified all of the FBI agents as graduates of Fordham University.

The FBI raid on St. Gregory's rectory had unanticipated consequences for Father Browne. The FBI background check on Browne (allegedly directed by his high school seminary classmate) revealed an aspect of Browne's life that was unknown to the parishioners of St. Gregory's parish. It turned out that Flavia Alaya, previously known only as a staunch supporter of the Strycker's Bay Neighborhood Council, had also been Browne's clandestine lover for the previous dozen years, and Browne—sixteen years her senior—was the father of her three children.

The FBI revelations of his relationship with Flavia Alaya forced him to resign as pastor of St. Gregory's in 1970. He died of leukemia on November 19, 1980, after his reconciliation with the Catholic Church, and he was buried with full honors from St. Gregory's Church. Alaya later wrote a candid account of her often difficult relationship with him, but local politicians and community leaders honored him by renaming West 90th Street between Amsterdam and Columbus avenues, the site of St. Gregory's Church, the Henry J. Browne Boulevard.[8]

Even during some of the most dangerous and depressing years in the history of the Upper West Side, Lyford sometimes caught a glimpse of another aspect of that part of New York City which many others had witnessed before and would have the opportunity to experience again. "Occasionally," he said,

> on a winter weekend the wind blows the smoke and sulphur dioxide over into New Jersey and presents the people of 105th Street with the gift of clear blue sky. If the weather is cold enough to drive the prostitutes and addicts under cover, we hear the birds in Central Park instead of the usual street obscenities. On a Sunday morning, with the schools closed, the street is quiet and almost deserted, at the end of the day we may have a crimson sunset at the end of the street, somewhere out beyond the Hudson River.[9]

"Everybody Got Mugged"

Joseph Lyford's sociological study of the Upper West Side in the 1960s is especially valuable as an outsider's professional view of the area. Almost fifty years later John Podhoretz, the editor of *Commentary*, confirmed much of Lyford's analysis, but he added his own reflections on Lyford's study from the perspective of someone who was a native of the Upper West Side and a witness to its rise, fall, and resurrection. Noting that it had been long touted as one of the most progressive neighborhoods in the United States, Podhoretz said that on the Upper West Side, "Social pathologies began to run rampant half a century ago, long before they broke into the wider culture."

Podhoretz mentioned that he was mugged four times before he was fourteen. It was nothing unusual. "Everybody got mugged." Once he was mugged as he was leaving the side door of the old Olympia movie theater at Broadway and 107th Street, down the block from Ascension Church. On that same block in 1972 a serial murderer repeatedly stabbed and mutilated a ten-year-old boy. Miraculously, the victim survived. Others were not so fortunate. The murderer roamed the neighborhood between 103rd and 106th streets in the vicinity of Broadway for a year, killing three other boys in the same vicious way. He was never apprehended. The city's major response to this crime wave was the massive urban renewal project between Central Park West and Amsterdam Avenue from West 87th Street to West 97th Street mentioned in the previous chapter, which resulted in the loss of 6,344 households. "The destruction and construction took years," said Podhoretz, echoing Henry Browne's complaints, "leaving behind rubble that became at-hand weaponry for kids and gangsters, and boarded-up tenements that became crime sites and drug dens."[10]

An addition to this urban renewal project was "Manhattantown, Inc.," a $54 million project between Central Park West and Amsterdam Avenue from West 97th Street to West 100th Street. In 1952 the Mayor's Slum Clearance Committee, headed by Robert Moses, sold this real estate, which was worth $15 million, to a private developer, Caspert and Company, for $1 million. Five years later, 280 of the 338 buildings slated for demolition were still standing amid the surrounding rubble, much to the satisfaction of Caspert and Company, which was collecting rent from the tenants in the decaying buildings while neglecting to pay city real estate taxes to the tune of $600,000. After a congressional investigation in 1957, Caspert and Company admitted that it was unable to develop the site, but not before two of the principal owners made a profit of a half-million dollars.[11]

Podhoretz bravely remained in the Upper West Side, where he raised his family and lived to see a better day. Writing in 2010, he said that, in the previous twenty years, the area had become "the most affluent *shtetl* the world has even seen." The Upper West Side is located in New York's 10th congressional district, which also includes most of the West Side and several neighborhoods in Brooklyn. In 2013 it was the most Jewish congressional district in the United States. One change for which Podhoretz was especially grateful was that his children would never have to learn, as he did, "how to accommodate and make normal an ever-present sense of everyday menace."[12]

The historian and journalist Theodore H. White, who lived in some of the most dangerous places in Europe after World War II, confessed that he was never afraid of going out at night until he moved to Central Park West and West 84th Street in 1953. A decade later Joseph Lyford examined the crime statistics in the 24th Precinct (which included the Upper West Side from 86th Street to 110th Street) for ten months in 1964. He tabulated 3,228 felonies, including 17 murders, 17 rapes, 388 assaults, 925 burglaries, and 1,241 instances of grand larceny.[13]

There was little continuity in the leadership of the NYPD in the 24th precinct, which included Ascension parish. "The captains of the 24th precinct appear and disappear as often as the people in the rooming houses," said Lyford, which made it difficult for them to put down roots in the neighborhood or win the confidence of local leaders. Lyford suspected that the police commissioner regarded the 24th precinct as a testing ground for the promotion of captains to inspectors. "If a captain handles this 'make-or-break' precinct satisfactorily, he is 'promoted out' and another candidate for inspector takes his place."[14]

For several decades thereafter, there were repeated complaints from residents that the city was using the Upper West Side as a dumping ground for drug addicts and pushers, the homeless, hoodlums, prostitutes, criminals, and mentally ill people. Lisa Lehr, the co-chairwoman of the West 90s/West 100s Neighborhood Coalition, told a magazine reporter in 1994 that "this area has become an open-air asylum." After a notorious local psychopath threw a marble bench through the windshield of her car, she announced, "We are not suicidal liberals anymore."[15]

Years later, Adam Gopnik traced some of the unforeseen political consequences of the crime wave that began to overwhelm many American cities, including New York, in the 1960s. "Liberal urbanists," he said, "who had been, perhaps mostly by chance, in power when the crime wave began, were discredited for a generation." He could not resist adding an impish comment, "The neo-cons gained credibility on foreign policy because they once seemed right about the Upper West Side."[16]

A Roman collar was no guarantee of safety, not at Ascension or at any neighboring parish on the Upper West Side. When a burglar broke into the rectory of Notre Dame Church at 114th Street and Morningside Drive, the pastor, Father Edward M.R. O'Brien, confronted him in the vestibule. The intruder attacked the elderly priest, bit him on his forehead, dashed out the front door, ran across the street, and disappeared into the darkness of

Morningside Park. At Holy Name rectory on West 96th Street, a burglar ordered a young associate pastor at gunpoint to empty out the cash in the parish safe for him. As the priest fumbled to remember the combination, the thief threatened to kill him instantly, if he did not act more quickly.

A Hint of a Future Spring

In 1963, as the Upper West Side was about to experience its protracted and devastating crime wave, the archdiocese assigned a new assistant pastor to Ascension, Father James Welby. Ordained only one year earlier, Father Welby was the ideal choice to be the new curate at Ascension. He was a native of the Upper West Side who had been deeply involved in both Ascension and Holy Name parishes as a teenager. Unlike most young Irish

Father James Welby, associate pastor of Ascension, 1962–69. (Photo courtesy of James Welby.)

Americans on the Upper West Side, he was fluent in Spanish long before he entered the major seminary at Dunwoodie.

It was a skill he first acquired as a student at Cathedral College, the archdiocesan minor seminary, a day school located on the Upper West Side at 87th Street and West End Avenue. He perfected his Spanish playing baseball with local Puerto Rican pick-up teams, where he was exposed to a more extensive and expressive command of the language than he would have acquired in a classroom at a university in New York City or Puerto Rico.

In the fall of 1963 Father Welby organized a Spanish-language parish mission in Ascension, a Spanish-language version of the traditional American parish mission that involved an intensive round of religious services designed to deepen the faith of practicing Catholics and to attract fallen-away Catholics back to the fold. A Sister of Charity, probably the principal of Ascension school, marveled at the meticulous way that Father Welby organized and promoted the mission. He distributed handbills advertising the mission from door-to-door in the parish, and at Ascension school and even in all the public schools in the parish.

He also employed a technique which was popular at that time with many politicians. He hired a van fitted out with a huge megaphone on the roof to travel up and down the streets of the parish advertising his recorded invitation to come to the mission. He even enlisted the members of the parish Catholic Youth Organization to act as babysitters so that their parents could attend the evening services.[17]

It is not clear how effective this Spanish mission was despite Father Welby's determined efforts to make it a success. However, it was a remarkable and prophetic affirmation of hope in the future of Ascension, a hint of a future spring, at a time when Ascension was beginning to descend into the bleak midwinter of its history.

9

Recovery and Renaissance

Hitting Rock Bottom

"Fortitude" has been defined as "courage for the long haul." It was an indispensable virtue for the survival of both the parish priests and the dwindling number of faithful parishioners at Ascension during the later decades of the twentieth century when the parish experienced the most difficult period in its century-long history. The demographic shift from a large active Irish Catholic community to an equally active but much smaller Hispanic Catholic community was reflected in the sacramental statistics.

Between 1961 and 1971 the number of practicing Catholics at Acension declined from 7,500 to 2,400, and 400 of them were children. Even more alarming was the number of nominal Catholics living within the parish boundaries, an estimated 22,000, of whom 4,600 were children. One cannot help but wonder how many of those children ever became practicing Catholics. By 1982 only 1,439 practicing Catholics were left in Ascension, little more than 10 percent of the number who had filled the pews at a dozen Masses every Sunday in the 1930s. Those statistics would remain virtually unchanged for the following 35 years.

Another notable sacramental statistic was the abrupt decline in confessions (a.k.a. the sacrament of reconciliation), a phenomenon that was not confined to Ascension by any means as a result of the widespread collapse of Tridentine-style devotional Catholicism in the wake of Vatican II. In 1932, an average of 2,600 parishioners went to confession every week. By 1994 that number had shrunk to 21 adults and nine children.[1]

By the mid-1970s the parish clergy consisted of only two permanently assigned priests—the pastor, Monsignor James Wilson, and an associate pastor, the Spanish-born Father Juan Plo. In the salad days of the 1930s and 1940s, Ascension could boast of five associate pastors, who were still called curates, to assist the pastor. The reduction in the size of the pastoral staff at Ascension made eminently good sense in view of the decline both in the number of parishioners in Ascension and the decline in the number of diocesan priests in the archdiocese of New York.

However, in 1976, the chairperson of the Ascension parish council, Ms. Mary S. Sanz, made an impassioned but respectful plea to the archdiocese to increase the number of priests at Ascension. "The parish itself is really mission territory," she explained, "and requires as many clergy as possible." The archdiocese took note of her request and the following year appointed Father John B. Sullivan to assist Monsignor Wilson as the administrator of Ascension, because Wilson was also the episcopal vicar for the Upper West Side.[2]

Ascension's problems were not limited to the diminishing numbers who frequented the doors of the church. The problems were aggravated by the fact that the church itself was located in a neighborhood that had become a center of the virulent crack-cocaine drug epidemic that plagued New York City in the 1980s. In 1988 a reporter for the *New York Times* identified the

Monsignor John B. Sullivan, administrator of Ascension, 1977–81. (Archives of the Archdiocese of New York.)

Upper West Side's two worst drug blocks as West 92nd Street and West 94th Street, a dozen blocks south of Ascension parish. Many of the dealers were local residents, which made it difficult for the police to apprehend them. "It's a war zone out there," complained one advertising executive who lived in the neighborhood. "The dealers are out on the street all night playing their boom boxes, fighting, screaming."[3]

The drug dealers were not fussy about the sites they selected for peddling their wares. One location was Straus Park, a mini-park located at Broadway and West 106th Street that had been established in 1915 as a memorial to Isidor Straus and his wife, Ida, prominent neighborhood residents, who had perished together in the sinking of the RMS *Titanic* three years earlier. Ida Straus famously refused the safety of a lifeboat to remain with her husband on the doomed *Titanic.* The drug dealers considered it amusing to hawk "family smokes" to young mothers pushing baby carriages or strollers through Straus Park.[4]

In 1990 there were 5,641 felonies recorded in the 24th police Precinct (which included the West Side of Manhattan from 86th Street to 110th Street), almost twice as many as 30 years earlier. They included 18 murders, 34 rapes, 1,193 robberies, 1,360 burglaries, 259 felonious assaults, 1,267 grand larcenies, and 1,510 grand larceny auto thefts. Not until the end of the decade was there a noticeable decline in the number of crimes.[5]

Writing in 2018 about this era in the recent history of New York City for those who had never experienced it, Adam Gopnik described the *mise-en-scène.* "[I]t's hard for those who did not live through the great crime wave of the sixties, seventies and eighties," he said, "to fully understand the scale or the horror of it, or the improbability of its end. Every set of blocks had its detours; a new arrival in New York was told always to carry a ten-dollar bill in case of a mugging. Crime ruled Broadway comedies: Neil Simon's *The Prisoner of Second Avenue* told the tale of people barricaded in their apartment for fear of muggings."

Gopnik mentioned the example of his own great-aunt and great-uncle, who lived on the Upper West Side at Riverside Drive and 115th Street. In 1962 they boasted of their upscale address; by 1975 they were afraid to invite visitors for fear that they would be mugged.[6]

The Coming of the Dominicans

A major reason for the survival and recovery of Ascension during the brutal crime wave that engulfed the Upper West Side was the influx into the parish of large numbers of families from the Dominican Republic at a time when many Puerto Rican families were leaving the parish.

In the late nineteenth and early twentieth centuries the United States often had a strained relationship with the Dominican Republic. In 1870 President Ulysses S. Grant tried to annex the Dominican Republic and use it as a refuge for recently emancipated American slaves. In a flagrant example of "gunboat diplomacy" in 1916, the United States began a military occupation of the country (and Haiti) that lasted for eight years. In 1965 the United States again invaded the Dominican Republic to prevent the installation of a left-wing government.

Two events in the 1960s made possible the massive immigration from the Dominican Republic to the United States. One was the assassination in 1961 of Rafael Trujillo, the military dictator of the Dominican Republic, who had strenuously blocked emigration to the United States for more than thirty years. The second event was the passage of the Hart–Celler Act of 1965, which vastly expanded quotas for immigration to the United States from the Western Hemisphere. Dominicans were among the principal beneficiaries of the Hart–Celler Act. At least 75 percent of these Dominican immigrants settled in New York City, especially in Washington Heights, where they numbered 40 percent of the total population by 1999.

Like earlier generations of European immigrants, many Dominicans found work in menial jobs, which, in twentieth-century New York City, often meant the service sector. Some showed impressive entrepreneurial skills. Men became "livery cab" drivers, a dangerous occupation in crime-ridden New York City, and Dominican women found ready employment in beauty parlors. Still other Dominicans also became famous as the proprietors of *bodegas*, tiny grocery stores in Hispanic neighborhoods. The *bodegas* were often family-operated enterprises like the familiar neighborhood Jewish candy stores of an earlier era. A typical *bodeguero* worked from early morning to late at night seven days a week. "I am a slave in this place," complained one of them.

The dream of many *bodegueros* was either to make a small fortune and return to the Dominican Republic or to establish their own independent supermarket in New York. The historian Tyler Anbinder has reminded us that not all Dominican immigrants were poor. There was also a considerable number of middle-class immigrants, including doctors, lawyers, and businessmen.[7]

The growth of the Dominican population in New York City was remarkable both for its size and its rapidity. In 1960 there were 111,000 Dominican immigrants in New York City. By 2000 their number had grown to 369,000, and they were the largest of the newly arrived immigrant groups in New York City. "In the Dominican Republic I was happy," said one immigrant, "but I had no future. In New York I have a lot of problems, but I have opportunity."[8]

The Dominicans achieved another milestone in New York City in 2013 when, for the first time, they outnumbered the Puerto Ricans by the margin of 747,473 to 719,444.[9]

Father Donald J. Johnston

In the summer of 1982, at the expiration of Monsignor Wilson's twelve-year term, Father Donald J. Johnston succeeded him as the pastor of Ascension. A native of Harrison, New York, in Westchester County, Father Johnston was ordained in 1955 and had spent all of his priestly ministry in predominantly Hispanic parishes in Manhattan, as an associate pastor, first at Holy Name Church on West 96th Street and later at the Church of the Incarnation in upper Manhattan, and then as pastor of the venerable Church of St. Teresa on the Lower East Side, the last church in the archdiocese blessed by Archbishop John Hughes before his death in 1864.

During his twelve years (1982–94) as pastor of Ascension, neither Father Johnston nor any other individual could do much to stem the crime wave that engulfed the neighborhood, but he was remembered affectionately by parishioners for encouraging them to maintain and strengthen their family bonds in an environment that was often indifferent, if not overtly hostile, to spiritual values of any kind.

One young English-speaking parishioner urged Father Johnston to make the English-language liturgy more appealing to young Catholics. "Our parish needs the young as well as the old," he said. "They are being lost." This same friendly critic urged Johnston to increase his efforts to unify the English and Hispanic communities, but he added candidly, "I am sure that this has been often discussed, and I have no ideas, but the problem is a big one." When this same parishioner was asked to evaluate the greatest strengths of the parish, he replied that the three greatest assets of the parish were "Father Johnson, Father Johnson, and Father Johnson [sic]."[10]

Based on attendance at Sunday Mass, it would appear that two-thirds of the active parishioners were Hispanic and the other third were mostly of Irish ancestry. However, during Father Johnston's twelve years at Ascension, a significant change began to manifest itself in the ethnic origins of the Hispanic community as numerous newcomers from the Dominican Republic settled in Ascension parish and eventually came to outnumber the older Puerto Rican community.

After completing his full twelve years as pastor of Ascension, Father Johnston declined to accept another assignment as pastor. Instead, he opted

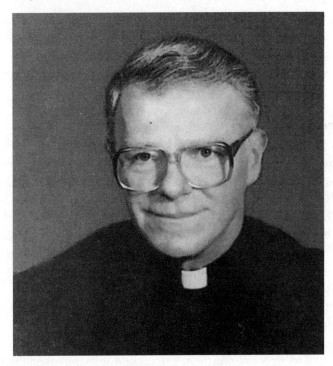

Father Donald J. Johnston, pastor of Ascension, 1982–94.
(Archives of the Archdiocese of New York.)

to become a full-time chaplain at Columbia–Presbyterian Medical Center in Washington Heights, where his fluency in Spanish proved to be an invaluable asset to both the patients and the pastoral staff. As a hospital chaplain, he continued to live in predominantly Hispanic local parishes until his retirement, when he moved to the St. John Vianney Clergy Residence in Riverdale. In 2019, at the age of eighty-nine, he was still traveling five days a week with the help of a cane by bus and subway from Riverdale to Columbia–Presbyterian Medical Center as an unpaid volunteer chaplain.

Father John P. Duffell

Father John P. Duffell became the eighth pastor of Ascension Church in July 1994 and was to remain as pastor for eighteen years, the third-longest tenure in Ascension's history after Monsignor Sweeny (1901–23) and Bishop Joseph Donahue (1924–59). A native of the Bronx who was ordained in 1969, Father Duffell had served previously as an associate pastor at Sacred Heart Church on West 51st Street and at St. Patrick's Church in Yorktown

Father John P. Duffell, pastor of Ascension, 1994–2012. (Photo courtesy of Fr. Duffell.)

Heights, and then as pastor of St. Peter's Church in Yonkers from 1981 to 1994. Both Sacred Heart and St. Peter's were predominantly Hispanic parishes, and Father Duffell came to Ascension as a fluent Spanish speaker able to minister to his largely Puerto Rican and Dominican parishioners in their native language.

A year after Father Duffell's arrival at Ascension, the parish celebrated its 100th anniversary. The proud new pastor boasted, "People call it the Big A." Sounding an optimistic note, he said, "The parish has a rich history around here. People are proud to be part of it. It has always been an activist parish—it's always had lots of people and lots of things going on."

A case in point was that, in 1995, when traditional parish societies like the Holy Name Society and the Rosary Altar Society had disappeared in many parishes, Ascension still had a functioning chapter of the Legion of Mary, an active charismatic prayer group, a program for teenagers and young adults called Buenos Amigos that had been in operation for fifteen years, and many dedicated lay members of the *Cursillo de Cristiandad*, an activist Catholic society that was extremely popular with many Hispanic Catholics.

Father Duffell also inherited from Father Johnston a parish with a growing involvement in community organizations. A local nonprofit agency ran a senior citizens' program at Ascension that provided lunch for 150 people every weekday. An Alcoholics Anonymous group met regularly in the parish center. Activities for young people included participation in the Boy Scouts and Cub Scouts, and a large basketball program. There was also an after-school program at Ascension school to serve neighborhood children.

Pastors in the archdiocese of New York have not been noted for tossing bouquets in the direction of either their predecessors or successors. How-ever, Father Duffell liked to say that he stood on Father Johnston's shoulders, and Father Johnston returned the compliment by saying that he could never have initiated the wide-ranging apostolate that Duffell developed at Ascension.[11]

The Ascension school itself struggled to survive with fewer than 300 students and the loss of the presence of both the Christian Brothers and the Sisters of Charity in the classrooms. When the lay principal unexpectedly resigned in 1995, Duffell asked his young associate pastor, Father Philip J. Kelly, to take his place. He did so and found it an exhilarating experience. "This is a little parish within a parish," said Father Kelly, "and it's a great experience, I've come to realize."[12]

Shortly thereafter, another crisis erupted in the school, when still another lay principal quit abruptly. Father Duffell found a replacement this time in a priest from Ireland, Father Sean McCaughley, who won the confi-dence of the faculty, parents, and students. He took pride in the fact that he knew every one of the students by name. As an associate pastor, McCaugh-ley was also instrumental in enhancing the quality of the liturgy, fostering discussion groups and developing the RCIA (Rite of Christian Initiation for Adults) program.

Another priest who made an invaluable contribution to Ascension was a priest from the Dominican Republic, Father Sixto Quezada. A native of the Dominican Republic, who was ordained for the archdiocese of Santo Domingo in 1983, he served as an associate pastor under both Father John-ston and Father Duffell from 1987 to 2011. The parishioners bestowed on him the affectionate nickname of Father Piro, as he is still known today as the pastor of the Church of Christ the King in the Bronx. More than anyone else, he was responsible for the organization of the thriving Hispanic com-munity at Ascension by fostering the Spanish-language liturgy and devel-oping Spanish-language pastoral programs. Father Duffell said of his efforts, "He did the work and I got the glory."[13]

In the course of its first one hundred years, the Church of the Ascension had experienced a number of renovations, some more enlightened and tasteful than others. Father Duffell made major changes in the interior of

Father Sixto Quezada (Father Piro), associate pastor of Ascension, 1987–2011. (Photo courtesy of Fr. Quezada.)

the church, restoring the pulpit to its original location, remodeling the sanctuary to reflect the aesthetics of the post–Vatican II liturgy, removing the ugly draperies that obscured the view of the original altar from the congregation, and, in the celebration of the liturgy, making greater use of the pipe organ that had been restored by Monsignor Curtin.

As the parishioners of Ascension were quick to notice, Father Duffell liked to organize elaborate liturgical celebrations to promote the unity of the parish. On Thanksgiving Day in 1996, he celebrated Mass for some 600 parishioners, many of them young people. Duffell blessed them as they walked in procession in front of the altar with their gifts of food for the needy. "The entire congregation brought something," said Father Duffell. "It was a flood of food."

One parishioner, Mr. Wigureto Pachecho, an usher and longtime parishioner, commented, "This is a unique day to thank God for what he has given us all year long, and also to share what we have with other people, especially needy people." The food collected at that Mass became part of a parish pantry that was used to feed poor people in the community.

Father Duffell was not shy about using the pulpit at Ascension to address contemporary social issues. At this Thanksgiving Day Mass in 1996, he focused his homily on immigration, noting how Ascension had evolved from a German and Irish parish to a predominantly Puerto Rican and Dominican parish. He described the Pilgrims as the "first immigrants" to these shores and offered a somewhat romanticized version of the friendly interaction between them and the Native Americans. However, an astute newspaper reporter sitting in the congregation got the point of the homily. "At times," he said, "the homily was a faintly veiled critique of the country's current attitude toward immigrants."[14]

Decline in Crime and Growth of Diversity

In 1990, New York City began a steady recovery from the crime wave that had made many neighborhoods virtually uninhabitable for thirty years or more. According to one expert, the drop in crime in New York City in the 1990s was "one of the most remarkable stories in the history of urban crime." He calculated that the recovery in New York City was more rapid and impressive than that in any other large American city.[15] The reasons for this decline remain elusive and contested according to one researcher, who said in 2016 that "the forces that drove the Great American Crime Decline remain a mystery."[16]

The sociologist Patrick Sharkey has offered the most convincing explanation to date for the sharp drop in crime across the United States. He attributed it to "the hard work of community groups combined with the enhanced presence of law enforcement, the criminal justice system, and private security forces." He suggests that New York City may lay claim to be "the poster child for the Great American Crime Decline." In the early 1990s, there were around 30 homicides for every 100,000 New Yorkers and

35 homicides for every resident of Newark. By 2014 the homicide rate in New York City was 4 per 100,000 while the homicide rate in Newark was 34 per 100,000.[17]

Community action played a significant role in the decline of crime and the preservation of many of the finest residential buildings on the Upper West Side. An especially important development was the conversion of many rental apartment buildings into "co-ops." James Panero, a native of the Upper West Side, explained that (in contrast to a condominium) in a co-op building "the residents are shareholders in a corporation that owns the entire building." The residents exercise their control through an elected co-op board.

Co-ops didn't become popular on the Upper West Side until the 1980s, but (together with the proliferation of owner-occupied condominiums) they had a transformative effect on the housing stock and the whole character of the neighborhood. As an eyewitness to and a participant in this transformation, Panero gave credit to the residents of the co-ops and their co-op boards. Writing in 2012, he said, "They have worked tirelessly to restore the beauty of the Upper West Side. Block by block, tree by tree, they have turned this neighborhood from a forsaken wreck into one of the most tranquil and desirable in the city."[18]

Whatever the exact reasons may have been, the Upper West Side was a prime beneficiary of the Great American Crime Decline. In the 24th Precinct, felonies declined from 5,641 in 1990 to 1,503 in 2001 and then leveled off to approximately 1,100 felonies annually for the next fifteen years. Between 1990 and 2016, felonies declined by 80.5 percent. In some categories the decline was even more impressive. There were 18 murders in 1990, but only one in 2016, a decline of 94.4 percent. Car thefts shrank from 1,510 in 1990 to 29 in 2016, an astonishing decline of 98.1 percent.

For the first time in decades it became possible to park a car on a street in the Upper West Side and expect to find it still there upon one's return. It was no longer necessary to post a sign in the window of a parked car with the plaintive message "No Radio Inside." By 2010 the Upper West Side was the second-safest neighborhood in Manhattan, outranked only by the more affluent and better-policed Upper East Side. In the 1980s more than 700 people were robbed every year in Central Park; in 2018 the annual number of robberies was in the teens and there had not been a murder in the park in fifteen years. Patrick Sharkey noted dryly that "homicide is a uniquely reliable measure of violent crime" because bodies are very hard to hide.[19]

The decline in crime not only improved the living conditions of the long-suffering residents of the Upper West Side, but it also made it an attractive neighborhood for upper-middle-class professional and business people. The result was a rash of renovations in stately pre-war (i.e., pre–World War II) apartment buildings and also the construction of new high-rise condominiums. One of the new luxury apartment buildings, Straus Park, was located on Broadway between West 106th Street and West 107th Street, overlooking the park and a stone's throw from Ascension Church.

While the decline in crime was a welcome change, one neighborhood leader, Robert Kupferstein, chairman of community board 7, had the courage to express concern that gentrification would erode the traditional Upper West Side commitment to social justice, especially for the poor. "Different concerns are coming to the fore," he warned. "Now that we have owner-occupied condos and co-ops," he explained, "we have people who are not concerned about solving the problems of the homeless for the sake of the homeless, but because it's a visual problem and property values are at stake."

Another community leader, the president of the Landmark West preservation group, who lived in the West 60s, viewed the rejuvenation of the Upper West Side from a different perspective and voiced alarm that soaring real estate values would attract a class of people whom she seemed to regard as politically undesirable and a threat to the Upper West Side's reputation as a liberal bastion. "All the new construction that's come to the neighborhood has brought a different type of person," she said. Giving a distinctly Upper West Side twist to the familiar *cri de coeur* of "There goes the neighborhood," she feared that "it's brought [in] a lot of Republicans."[20]

Ascension Redivivus

The decline in crime and changing demographics in the neighborhood also transformed Ascension into a more diverse parish community. As a result, Father Duffell redoubled his efforts to reach out to English-speaking parishioners as well as to Hispanics.

An inquisitive newspaper reporter visited Ascension in the spring of 2008. It was a time when the Catholic Church in the United States was grappling with declining numbers at Mass, a shortage of priests, and a devastating clerical sexual abuse scandal. She said that, in the midst of this crisis, "Ascension stands as just one example of a parish that remains a vibrant presence in the lives of its ever-changing—and still growing—congregation." This reporter attended three Sunday Masses: a lively Spanish liturgy, an elegant English-language Mass, and a rousing Sunday evening jazz Mass attended largely by several hundred young people. As a result of this experience, she categorized Ascension with admiration as three different congregations united within one parish.

Father Duffell told her, "We have a great richness in the city here, in our neighborhood, and that has to be reflected in our parish, in our worship. You have to observe and respond to what you have and see." A woman from the Dominican Republic, Ms. Altagracia Hiraldo, who had been a parishioner at Ascension for thirty years, echoed Father Duffell's comments. She welcomed the fact that the parish had changed "100 percent." "We did not have enough people," she said. "There were no Americans [sic], just Dominicans and maybe some Puerto Ricans. Now it is everybody: Americans, Peruvians, Mexicans, Ecuadoreans, everyone."

Among the people whom Father Duffell welcomed to Ascension every Sunday were lesbian, gay, bisexual, and transgender Catholics. Thirty years earlier, in a very different atmosphere, another Upper West Side pastor, Father Henry Browne, had allowed the Gay Liberation Front to use the rectory of St. Gregory's Church for their meetings, but he warned them not to advertise them.[21]

At Ascension, under Father Duffell, the weekly parish bulletin contained the announcement: "No matter your age, your race, your gender or sexual orientation, there is a place for you at Ascension." It was a message that he repeated every Sunday from the pulpit. One gay parishioner, John Gasdaska, a forty-three-year old real estate agent, commented, "The simple fact that he includes talking openly about that makes a world of difference." For him it was an assurance that "there is just no question that everyone is included in the message of Christ."[22]

Ascension under Father Dufell was not the only Catholic parish in New York City that extended a cordial welcome to LGBT Catholics. The Jesuits at the Church of St. Francis Xavier on West 16th Street had a long reputation of being equally hospitable. So did the Church of St. Joseph in Greenwich Village under Father Also Tos, who held weekly meetings with gay and lesbian parishioners for prayer and discussions. When Tos organized the Millennium Lecture Series at St. Joseph's to commemorate 2,000 years of Christian history, one of the speakers was Andrew Sullivan, the English-born former editor of The New Republic, who boldly called his talk, "We're Here: Homosexuals and the Catholic Church."[23]

Never shy about expressing his opinions to those in high places, Tos engaged in an ongoing dialogue with both Cardinal John O'Connor and the vicar general, Bishop Patrick J. Sheridan, about pastoral ministry to LGBT Catholics in which he emphasized the necessity of listening to their lived experience. On June 28, 1997, Bishop Sheridan celebrated Mass for the LGBT community in St. Joseph's Church and remained after the Mass for a lengthy discussion period. The church was filled. Tos assured Cardinal

O'Connor that "everything was both pastorally sensitive and faithful to the teachings of the Church."[24]

Father Duffell remained as pastor of Ascension for eighteen years (1994–2012), six years beyond the usual term limit for a pastor in the archdiocese of New York. He left Ascension in 2012 to move to the Church of the Blessed Sacrament on West 71st Street, where he succeeded Monsignor Robert B. O'Connor as pastor and continued with undiminished enthusiasm his widely admired, if sometimes unconventional, ministry to the people of another Upper West Side Catholic community.

10

Father Daniel S. Kearney

In July 2012 Father Daniel S. Kearney replaced Father Duffell as pastor of Ascension. A native of Poughkeepsie, New York, he was fluent in Spanish, as were his three immediate predecessors. Father Kearney had spent his first four years after his ordination in 1987 as an associate pastor at Holy Family Church in the Bronx. His first two pastorates, Our Lady Queen of Martyrs in Inwood and St. Elizabeth's in Washington Heights, were large

Father Daniel S. Kearney, pastor of Ascension, 2012–present. (Photo courtesy of Fr. Kearney.)

and flourishing Hispanic parishes most of whose parishioners traced their ancestry to the Dominican Republic.

His appointment as pastor of Queen of Martyrs in 1991 raised many an envious clerical eyebrow because of his age. He was only twenty-nine years old and had been ordained only four years. It was quite unusual for such a young priest to be appointed a pastor at that time in the archdiocese of New York, where it had long been customary for a priest to wait twenty-five years or more to become a pastor.

At Ascension, Father Kearney faced a different and more substantial challenge than in his two previous pastorates, as he candidly admitted. It was his first experience as pastor of a multiethnic and multicultural parish community. Father Duffell had been instrumental in reaching out to these diverse Anglo and Hispanic communities, including LGBT Catholics, and made them feel welcome at Ascension. Father Kearney continued this encouragement of inclusiveness and diversity at Ascension. He felt especially empowered to do so after Cardinal Timothy Michael Dolan, who became archbishop of New York in 2009, told him, at the time of his appointment as pastor of Ascension, that Father Duffell had made many people feel welcome at Ascension and he wanted Father Kearney to continue that policy.

A Parish Profile in 2017

In 2012, Sunday Mass attendance at Ascension had remained remarkably stable for the previous thirty-five years: 1,439 people in 1982 and 1,427 people in 2013.[1] The days when parishes in Manhattan like Ascension's could boast of 10,000 parishioners or more at Sunday Mass were now a distant memory unlikely to return until (to use a crude Soviet-era comparison) pigs learned to fly and shrimp began to whistle. To become the pastor of Ascension or of many other urban parishes in the archdiocese of New York in 2012 was not for the faint-of-heart or for any priest lamenting the demise of old-fashioned Irish-American Catholicism in New York City.

During Father Kearney's first four years at Ascension, Sunday Mass attendance declined from 1,427 in 2013 to 1,175 in 2015 and then rebounded to 1,299 in 2017. Father Kearney's pastoral approach was focused on two interrelated aspects of Catholic spirituality: the central importance of the liturgy and the need to implement on the parish level the well-established principles of Catholic teaching on social justice.

Ascension was now essentially a one-priest parish, although the pastoral staff was augmented by two resident priests, Father Raymond Rafferty, the retired pastor of Corpus Christi Church, and Father Daniel LeBlanc, O.M.I., a staff member at the New York office of Catholic Relief Services, who was fluent in Spanish after spending thirty years as a missionary in Peru. There was also an additional priest on alternate Sundays and priests from the Dominican Republic during the summer months. Two laymen also played an important role in the pastoral staff: Mr. Warren Thomas, the hospital chaplain, and Mr. Cipriano Lantigua, a veteran parishioner, who served as the director of the Ministry for the Sick and the Homebound.

There were seven weekend Masses, four in English and three in Spanish. Attendance at the Spanish-language Masses outnumbered that at the English-language Masses by a margin of 766 to 533. These statistics give a misleading underestimate of the overwhelmingly Hispanic character of the parish in 2012 because many bilingual Hispanic parishioners now attended the English-language Masses. In fact, long before 2012, Ascension had become a predominantly Hispanic parish composed largely but not exclusively of Spanish-speaking immigrants from the Dominican Republic and their American-born children and grandchildren. In 2017 half of the baptisms and marriages and most of the funerals in the parish were celebrated in Spanish.

Like many progressive post–Vatican II pastors, Father Kearney compensated for the decline in the number of full-time parish priests at Ascension by fostering a wider involvement of the laity in the pastoral life of the parish. There was an elected parish council and an active finance council. There were also more than two dozen lay-run organizations. They ran the gamut from well-established traditional groups such as the Altar Servers Society, the bilingual Legion of Mary, and the St. Vincent de Paul Society to newer groups like the Ascension Food Pantry, Ascension Gay Fellowship, and Martini Night Fellowship. Hispanic Catholics were well represented by the Cursillistas, the Cofradia de la Altagracia, and the Hermandad del Sagrado Corazon de Jesus, to mention only a few of the Spanish-language parish societies.

The Celebration of the Liturgy in Ascension Church

The Second Vatican Council (1962–65) set in motion many far-reaching changes in the Catholic Church. The most obvious change on the parish level was the way that Catholics worshipped at Mass. Priests now celebrated Mass in the language of the people, not in Latin, and the laity were invited to participate actively in the celebration of the liturgy. The degree of active participation by the laity varied from parish to parish, depending upon the whim of the pastor and the desire of the bishop. Cardinal McIntyre thought that lay participation in the liturgy was a distraction. Ascension was one of many parishes that embraced enthusiastically the liturgical reforms of

Vatican II. Father Kearney inherited this legacy at Ascension and was eager to preserve and develop it.

Prior to Vatican II, many parishes, especially Irish-American parishes, skimped on providing music at Mass. Even well-attended Sunday Masses were often celebrated without any musical accompaniment. "Catacombical liturgy," Father Walter Elliott, a Paulist priest, called the practice caustically in the early twentieth century, an allusion to the way that the early Christians were alleged to have worshipped in the underground cemeteries in Rome. At Ascension, however, there were a full-time organist, director of music, and choirmaster, Mr. Preston Smith, M. M., and music and a cantor at all the Sunday Masses. The 11 o'clock Mass was a choral Mass, which an earlier generation of Catholics would have called a "High Mass" with a robed choir and an extensive repertoire of classical and contemporary liturgical music.

The Hispanic community took charge of their own music at the Spanish-language Masses. The 9:30 Mass on Sunday morning was the lively Spanish-language counterpart of the more sedate English-language choral Mass. It was run by the Walkirios, a Hispanic musical ensemble that featured popular Spanish and Latin American hymns accompanied by the piano, guitars, and drums celebrated at a decibel level that did not require electronic amplification, which was also true of the enthusiastic singing of the congregation. The Walkirios had a long and distinguished history in the parish. They were founded in October 1968 by five dedicated lay people: José Fermin, Melba Fermin, Pedro Peña, Aurora Sanchez, and José Baez, the last of whom continued to serve as the director in 2019.

At both the English- and Spanish-language liturgies, the participation of the laity as lectors, altar servers, Eucharistic ministers, and ushers was impressive. In 2017 there were ninety lectors, eighty Eucharistic ministers, twenty ushers, and seventeen altar servers. Women outnumbered men in these ministries by a margin of two to one, except for the ushers. In the sanctuary, altar servers executed their functions with flawless efficiency and grace thanks to the dedication of the erudite Mr. Michael Elmore, the parish coordinator who did double duty as the overworked parish sacristan.

The most recent and innovative of the Sunday liturgies at Ascension was established by Father Duffell in the late 1990s and was celebrated on Sunday evening at 6:00, except during the summer months. It was referred to as the "Jazz Mass" because of the music, which was deliberately chosen to appeal to young Catholics and attracted almost 200 of them every week. On the first Sunday of each month the Jazz Mass was followed by a pot-luck supper accompanied by a variety of adult beverages. It accidentally acquired another name when an irate parishioner objected to the music and referred to the liturgy disparagingly as the "Martini Mass." The name went viral and spread throughout the archdiocese as a term of approval and admiration.[2]

Liturgy in the widest sense in the Catholic tradition includes not only the celebration of the Eucharist but also the celebration of the sacraments. The sacrament of reconciliation (confession) was available every Saturday afternoon at Ascension in both Spanish and English, but there were also communal celebrations of the sacrament of reconciliation twice a year, each of which was attended by more than 150 people. Likewise, the sacrament of the anointing of the sick was always available upon request, but twice a year there was also a communal celebration of that sacrament at which some 100 people were anointed.[3]

Catholic Education

In the mid–nineteenth century, New York's first archbishop, John Hughes, emphasized the vital importance of Catholic education when he said in a pastoral letter in 1850 that "the time is almost come when it will be necessary to build the school-house first and the parish church afterwards."[4] Successive archbishops of New York, taking advantage of the abundant supply of religious sisters and brothers, continued to expand the parochial school system at a furious pace for the following one hundred years. As was already mentioned, when Ascension school opened its doors in 1912, it was one of ten new parochial schools that were established that year. A century later it was increasingly difficult, if not impossible, for many parishes to maintain their parochial schools for financial and other reasons.

In 2017, Ascension School remained open with an enrollment of 302 students, but it was now a regional school, which meant that many of the students came from outside the parish. For the Ascension students in public schools there was a catechetical program with an enrollment of 127 students that was designed to meet the individual needs of young people at every stage of their religious development from pre-kindergarten to high school. There were 22 different classes in both English and Spanish, including special-needs classes taught by certified special-education teachers. The classes took place on Sunday morning in the school followed by attendance at the 11:00 Mass. There were additional classes on Saturday afternoon from 3:30 to 5:00, followed by attendance at the 5:00 evening Mass.

"The key element is formation, not just education," said Ms. Robin Brooks Klueber, the Director of Religious Education, who developed this innovative program. She explained that the students "are encouraged to develop their own individual relationship with Christ and to become His disciples." As a practical way of putting their faith into practice, many of the older students participated in the operation of the Ascension Food Pantry and the Ascension Homeless Shelter.[5]

Catholics worldwide increasingly recognized that religious education needed to include adults as well as children. At Ascension there were several retreat programs for teenagers and young adults. The parish also sponsored its own Rite of Christian Initiation for Adults (RICA) program, an enormously popular national program for converts and nominal Catholics who wished to participate fully in the sacramental life of the Church. In terms of numbers, the most successful program of religious education at Ascension was the series of instructional sessions for parents and godparents of the children who were about to receive baptism, First Communion, the Sacrament of Reconciliation, and confirmation. In 2017 almost 600 parents were involved in these programs.[6]

Parish Finances and Improvements

Between 2010 and 2017, annual parish expenses always amounted to well over $1 million, from a low of $1,048,552 in 2011 to high of $1,212,630 in 2013. However, in those same years there was a steady increase in revenue from $777,899 in 2010 to $1,086,553 in 2017. As a result, the deficit decreased from $312,308 in 2010 to $44,030 in 2017. The principal source of income at Ascension, as in most parishes, was the Sunday and holyday collections, supplemented by fundraising programs that raised a total of $515,645.66 in 2017. Other important sources of income were the rental of church properties to outside organizations, donations, and bequests.

As a result of the improvement in parish finances, Father Kearney was able to make a considerable number of repairs and improvements to the church, school, and rectory. Some of them were essential maintenance items in century-old buildings such as replacing and repairing the roof in the church and rectory, undertaking the mandatory pointing of the exterior walls of the school, replacing the sidewalk vaults in front of the church and the rectory, installing security cameras, and providing separate new boilers for the church and rectory. Many of these improvements may have escaped the attention of most parishioners, but one amenity that was widely noticed and appreciated was the installation of air conditioning in the church.[7]

Social Justice and the Mission to the Dominican Republic

Mention has already been made of the vibrant state of the liturgy at Ascension. With regard to social justice, the century-old parish branch of the St. Vincent de Paul Society continued its apostolate of providing financial assistance to needy families. More recently, Father Kearney established the weekly Ascension Food Pantry and a homeless shelter that coordinates its work with municipal social service agencies to provide overnight lodging two nights a week not only in the winter but also during nine months a year. The success of all of these endeavors was made possible by the generosity of lay volunteers who staffed the homeless shelter.

One of the most impressive features of Ascension's commitment to social justice has been the Mission to the Dominican Republic, which consists of a week-long visit to a different rural area of that country each year. Father Kearney was quick to point out that the initiative for this Mission did not originate with him. He gave the credit to two young New York priests of Dominican ancestry, Father Ambiorix Rodriguez and Father Joseph Espaillat, who were his associate pastors when he was the pastor of the Church of Mary Queen of Martyrs in Inwood. Father Rodriguez began the mission with Father Kearney's blessing in 1997, and Father Espaillat continued it.

After Father Espaillat's reassignment to another parish, Father Kearney assumed the direction of the Mission himself. When he became the pastor of St. Elizabeth's Church in Washington Heights, he introduced the Mission to that parish, where it was well received. Upon his appointment as pastor of Ascension in 2012, he continued the Mission at Ascension at the request of parishioners who had heard of its success at Queen of Martyrs and St. Elizabeth's. The annual Mission today, headed by Father Kearney, includes both parish volunteers as well as doctors and dentists and other health care professionals and provides a full complement of spiritual and medical services to some of the poorest residents of the Dominican Republic.

Aggiornamento: Upper West Side Style

The origins of the liturgical revival in Europe and the United States predate Vatican II by several decades. One of the pioneers of this revival on the local level was a Manhattan pastor, Father George Barry Ford, the pastor of Corpus Christi Church on West 121st Street from 1934 until 1958 and the chaplain to the Catholic students at Columbia University. In the 1930s, when Mass was still celebrated in Latin, at Corpus Christi a second priest stood in the pulpit during Mass leading the congregation in the recitation of the English translation of the Latin text (except for the Eucharistic Prayer) for the benefit of the congregation.

Like pioneers of the liturgical revival, both in Europe and the United States, Father Ford was a firm believer in the essential association of good liturgy with social justice. He practiced what he preached by pledging the support of his parish for a neighborhood urban renewal project. Ford's advocacy of a vernacular liturgy and his sponsorship of social justice projects earned him the reputation of a clerical maverick from critics in high places in the archdiocese of New York.

He was chastised for celebrating Compline, the official night prayer of the Church, in English rather than in Latin. Incredibly, when he sent a bouquet of Easter lilies to Riverside Church on the occasion of the tenth anniversary of their new church, Monsignor J. Francis McIntyre, the chancellor of the archdiocese, asked him, "Is this not a manifestation of 'brotherhood' that borders on *communicatio [in sacris]*?" the official canonical term for participation in non-Catholic worship.[8]

When McIntyre was appointed the archbishop of Los Angeles on February 7, 1948, many New York priests called the train that took him on the first leg of his journey to California the "Freedom Train." It was not only a sardonic expression of their relief at his departure, but also a none-too-subtle reference to the Freedom Train sponsored by the U.S. government that toured the entire country from 1947 to 1949, exhibiting precious historical documents from the National Archives. One of the documents in the traveling exhibit was the Emancipation Proclamation.

Monsignor McIntyre was not the only diocesan official who tried to censure Father Ford. In 1951, the vicar general, Monsignor Edward R. Gaffney, demanded that Ford submit for his inspection copies of the sermons preached in Corpus Christi Church.

The feisty Father Ford refused to do so. He told Gaffney, "Permit me to add that, when I know that the most essential needs of your own parish have cried long for attention, one rebels against prescriptions that need home consumption. I am fully aware that a sweet reply would be infinitely more politic, but that adoption is the invariable choice of dishonesty and cowardice."

In an inspired example of preventive one-upmanship, Ford informed Gaffney that he was sending a copy of his letter to Cardinal Spellman.[9]

A few years later, another vicar general, Monsignor John Maguire, forbade Ford from speaking at a meeting of the New York Teachers' Guild. Ford obeyed the order, but he told Maguire that he had "instant respect for the historic and important office you hold." However, he warned Maguire that "when it becomes a police station where suspects report, it no longer enjoys esteem."[10]

Ford was a pioneer in starting a parish bulletin to eliminate lengthy pulpit announcements. He also inaugurated a monthly newsletter, the *Corpus Christi Chronicle*, which made available short essays by some of the best American and European Catholic writers. In 1936, in the middle of the Great

Depression, he built a new combination church-and-school. Unlike many such structures, Corpus Christi Church really looked like a church, with splendid stained-glass windows and tasteful interior appointments. Ford was acutely aware that there were eight world-famous institutions located within the boundaries of his parish. In asking Cardinal Hayes for permission to build a new church, he said, "This is not just another parish, but a strategically situated one where the best that the Church can do ought to be done."[11]

One of the eight world-famous institutions located within the boundaries of Corpus Christi parish was Teachers College of Columbia University. Many Catholic educators regarded Teachers College with fear and loathing because they considered it to be the citadel of the kind of "progressive education" they associated with John Dewey. Father Ford adopted a more nuanced position.

When he noticed women religious in full pre–Vatican II religious habits studying for graduate degrees at Teachers College, he inquired about the identity of a congregation of women religious that had the temerity to send their young sisters to Teachers College. When he discovered that they were Dominican Sisters of Sinsinawa, Wisconsin, he quickly obtained their services for his own parochial school, where they set new standards of academic excellence in the elementary schools of the archdiocese of New York.[12]

Father Leo J. O'Donovan, S.J., the distinguished Jesuit theologian and President Emeritus of Georgetown University, who grew up in Corpus Christi parish in the 1940s, was a witness as a young man to the transformation of the parish under Father Ford. He described Ford as "one of the heroes of my life" and said that "it would take another lifetime for me to express even somewhat adequately my gratitude to Corpus Christi." As for the Sinsinawa Dominicans in Corpus Christi school, Father O'Donovan said that they "changed my life forever . . . In effect they took the best of John Dewey and blessed us children with it."[13]

Although Ford was *persona non grata* in the New York chancery office, he won widespread praise from many of his own parishioners and from priests far beyond the borders of his own parish. Father Ford's successors as pastors of Corpus Christi, including Monsignor Myles Bourke, Monsignor Patrick Carney, Father Raymond Rafferty, and others, continued his commitment to good liturgy and social justice as a legacy to the Catholics of the Upper West Side. This double legacy received a warm welcome at the Church of the Ascension, first under Father Duffell and later under Father Kearney. Both of them made it a cornerstone of their own pastoral ministry.

The Bishop and the Pacifist

Perhaps the only liberal Catholic in New York City who regretted McIntyre's departure for the Golden State in 1948 was, of all people, Dorothy Day, the co-founder of the Catholic Worker Movement. One of her admirers, J. M. Cameron, went so far as to say that Dorothy Day loved McIntyre (who became an auxiliary bishop of New York in January 1941) despite the fact that she disagreed with him on virtually every topic under the sun. Cameron attributed her magnanimity to the fact that "she never failed in charity toward those who were farthest from her." The scope of her charity included even Cardinal Spellman, who was the *bête noir* of many American liberal Catholics.[14]

However, the friendly relationship between McIntyre and Dorothy Day was not based solely on Dorothy Day's generous charity toward him. McIntyre came to recognize her as an authentically holy person, even though her sanctity was of a somewhat unconventional variety, and he admired her fervent commitment to the poor. In response to a query from Archbishop Amleto Cicognani, the Apostolic Delegate to the United States, about Dorothy Day and the *The Catholic Worker*, McIntyre said,

> She is an ardent convert, a daily communicant and zealously fighting, according to her mind, for true principles of justice. . . . The sincerity of herself and her group is manifested in that they strive to live a Franciscan life of poverty and simplicity.[15]

The most controversial aspect of Dorothy Day's spirituality during World War II was her uncompromising pacifism, which outraged many American Catholics, including Cardinal Spellman, the military vicar for the armed forces. It even produced numerous schisms within the Catholic Worker Movement.[16] To Dorothy Day's dismay, draft boards commonly rejected efforts of Catholics to be classified as conscientious objectors on the basis of their religious convictions. They justified their refusal on the grounds that, unlike the Quakers and the Mennonites, Catholics could not claim that pacifism was a tenet of their religion.

On this issue Dorothy Day found an unlikely ally in McIntyre. He enlisted the services of Monsignor William R. O'Connor, a respected theologian at St. Joseph's Seminary, Dunwoodie, who declared that there was ample justification in Catholic theology for a Catholic to claim to be a conscientious objector on the basis of his or her religion. "It seems to me," O'Connor told McIntyre, "that any Catholic, or group of Catholics, [is] perfectly within their rights in taking a pacifistic stand in regard to waging war.

Undated handwritten letter from Dorothy Day to Archbishop
McIntyre. (Retention Center of the Archdiocese of New York,
St. Joseph's Seminary.)

The civil law itself recognizes this and there is nothing in our moral theology or ethical principles against it."

Monsignor O'Connor added a special plea for Dorothy Day and the Catholic Worker movement. "I feel they are doing God's work down on Mott Street and I hope that will not have to suffer too much for standing by their principles in these difficult times. . . . I earnestly beg your Excellency to be

as gentle with them as is possible." McIntyre replied that he had no intention of taking any action against them. "I now feel armed by your argument
and shall be ready for all oncomers."[17]

Father Francis P. Duffy

A half-century before Father Ford, there was another West Side pastor
(albeit not an *Upper* West Side pastor) who articulated many of the theological views that would later be identified with liberal Catholicism as it was
practiced by many Upper West Side Catholics. He was Father Francis P.
Duffy, pastor of Holy Cross Church on West 42nd Street, the former chaplain of the N.Y. 69th Regiment in World War I.

Duffy's fame as a military chaplain has obscured his earlier career as a
young and creative theology professor at the New York diocesan seminary
at Dunwoodie, where he was one of the founders of the short-lived *New York
Review*. The subtitle of the *Review* indicated its purpose: "A Journal of the
Ancient Faith and Modern Thought." Duffy once said, "The faith does not
change and does not need to change, but we must find new approaches to
it and new ways of presenting it." If those words sound familiar and reso-
nate with many Upper West Side Catholics today, it may be because they
are almost exactly the same words that Pope John XXIII used in his address
at the opening of Vatican II. But Duffy wrote those words sixty years before
Vatican II.[18]

More than a half-century ago, Duffy also said, "Lack of faith is not our
difficulty, unless it be that worst form of infidelity which fears to look at the
truth. Our main drawback," he added, "is a certain intellectual sloth which
masquerades as faith." Duffy was not content to deplore the status quo. He
called for *aggiornamento* long before it became a popular theological term.
"We need men of faith," he explained, "men who will not call the counsel of
their own little prejudices sacrosanct . . . but men, who in [John] Locke's
expressive phrase 'have raised themselves above the alms-basket and are
not content to live lazily on scraps of begged opinions.'"

Few Catholic seminary professors of his day quoted John Locke or even
knew who he was. For his efforts Duffy was quietly dismissed from the
faculty of Dunwoodie in 1912 and sent to establish a new parish in a poor
Bronx neighborhood where, Duffy said, there was not a single person with
a college education. A year later Cardinal Farley described Duffy to a Vatican
official as one who "has shown for years a strong leaning to the liberal
tendency of the time called Modernism."[19] Both the U.S. government and
the French government honored Duffy for his service in World War I, but
his own Church never even made him a monsignor, probably because of the

Father Francis P. Duffy, chaplain of the 69th New York Regiment, and Cardinal
Patrick Hayes. (Author's personal collection.)

lingering taint of liberalism. The snub did not seem to bother Duffy. He said
that the title he valued most was simply "Father Duffy."

After the war, when Duffy redoubled his efforts to promote Irish independence from British rule, he also used the opportunity to reaffirm his
commitment to liberal values, especially freedom of speech. During a lecture

in Carnegie Hall on February 25, 1921, during the War of Irish Independence, irate Irish Americans mercilessly heckled the speaker, Sir Philip Gibbs, because, with good reason, they considered Gibbs to be a slick British propagandist. There was a heavy police presence, but the cops all seemed to be of a certain ethnic background. They just smiled at the hecklers and occasionally waved a disapproving finger at them. "Ninety Minutes of Uproar" was the headline in one New York newspaper the next morning.

Duffy was sitting in the audience with a handkerchief concealing his Roman collar. In the midst of the pandemonium, Duffy jumped up onto the stage, identified himself as Father Duffy, grabbed the microphone from Gibbs, and defended Gibbs's right to be heard. Duffy explained his action a short time later. "My personal idea of well-ordered liberty," he said "is most admirably and succinctly indicated by the taunting imperative of childhood days, 'Go and hire a hall.' It contains in brief all of my ideas about free speech." Given that Gibbs had hired a hall, Duffy concluded that his critics had two options open to them. They could either take him to court or hire a hall themselves, but they had no right to disrupt his lecture.[20]

Accidentally but fortunately, Father Duffy had the opportunity to make one last contribution to American Catholic theology as a West Side pastor during the presidential campaign of 1928. New York Governor Alfred E. Smith, the Democratic candidate and the first Catholic major-party nominee for the presidency, came under attack because of his religion. In an article in the *Atlantic Monthly*, Charles Marshall, an Episcopalian layman and constitutional lawyer, claimed that a conscientious Catholic could not serve as President of the United States because he would have to place the authority of papal encyclicals above that of the Constitution of the United States. When he saw the article, Governor Smith supposedly said, "What the hell is an encyclical?" He then asked Father Duffy to help him compose a response to Marshall.

Father Duffy was happy to do so. Al Smith's response, which appeared in the subsequent issue of the *Atlantic Monthly*, was a resounding success. The words were Smith's, but the ideas were Duffy's. Duffy used essentially the same argument that Father John Courtney Murray, S.J., was to use thirty years later. Duffy argued that there had been a development of the Church's doctrine on religious liberty, and that the Church's earlier teachings on the union of church and state and the need to restrict religious freedom of non-Catholics, were no longer applicable in the modern world, least of all in the United States. Duffy told Marshall through the pen of Governor Smith, "I think that you have taken your thesis from [the] limbo of defunct controversies."[21]

Publicly, Duffy minimized his role in the controversy. Privately, he told a different story. He confided to a prominent New York lawyer who was a personal friend, "I have held very ardent convictions on these matters since I was nineteen years of age, and it was a matter of keen joy to me to take advantage of Governor Smith's prestige to win a victory over the opposing Catholic school of thought."[22] Unknown to Governor Smith and Father Duffy, Cardinal Patrick Hayes sent a copy of Smith's article to Rome, where Cardinal John Bonzano, the former apostolic delegate to the United States, pronounced it a *capo lavoro*, "a masterpiece." Moreover, Bonzano added, "it was judged such by everybody here who knows conditions in America."[23]

As a West Side pastor from 1920 to 1932, Duffy became the Catholic Church's premier ambassador of good will to New Yorkers of all religions and none. Improbably, one of his warmest admirers was Alexander Woollcott, the acerbic drama critic and journalist, an outspoken atheist, who first met Chaplain Duffy as a war correspondent in France and took an instant liking to him because of what Woollcott said was his "genial missions *in partibus infidelium*," meaning his nonjudgmental outreach to nonbelievers like himself. After the war, Woollcott called him "the great New Yorker." He explained that

> when he walked down the street—any street—he was like a *curé* striding through his own village. Everyone knew him. I have walked beside him and thought that I had never seen so many *pleased* faces. . . . Father Duffy was of such dimensions that he made New York into a small town.

Standing amid the crowds on the steps outside St. Patrick's Cathedral for Duffy's funeral, Woollcott overheard a policeman tell a woman that she would have to move. "But, officer," protested the woman, "I was a personal friend of Father Duffy." "Madam," replied the officer, "everyone here today was a personal friend of Father Duffy." "The policeman's answer was an epitaph," said Woollcott.[24]

Plus ça Change . . .

For 200 years two dynamics have exercised a powerful influence in shaping the nature of New York Catholicism. They are immigration and neighborhood change.

The Catholic Church in New York City has always been "The Immigrant Church," in the words of the historian Jay Dolan.[25] The only variable has been the place of origin of the immigrants. Father Charles Whelan, the pastor of New York City's first Catholic church, St. Peter's, Barclay Street, in lower Manhattan, reported in 1785 that six languages were spoken by his tiny congregation of 200 people: English, French, Dutch [i.e., German], Spanish, Portuguese, and Irish.[26]

Over the course of the following two centuries, successive waves of immigrants from Italy, eastern Europe, Puerto Rico, the Dominican Republic, Mexico, the Caribbean, Central America, Africa, and Asia further increased the ethnic diversity of the New York Catholic community. In 2008, Mass was celebrated in the archdiocese of New York every Sunday in thirty-three languages, including Akan, Arabic, Igbo, and Tagalog.

The other powerful dynamic that has shaped the nature of New York Catholicism has been the never-ending fluctuations of the economic and social character of local neighborhoods as they have shifted from upscale to poor and to upscale again, from residential to commercial and residential again, and from white to black and white again, the last of which is evident in the contemporary gentrification of central Harlem.

A striking example of the unpredictable gyrations in the lucrative New York real estate market is the varying fortunes of New York's first Catholic church, St. Peter's, Barclay Street. In 1896, a century after its establishment, the pastor, Monsignor James McGean, complained that he had recently lost 500 parishioners. "Brooklyn and [New] Jersey have taken away our industrious middle class," he said. One of the vicars general, Monsignor Joseph Mooney, recommended closing the church and selling the property to pay for the new seminary at Dunwoodie. Fortunately his advice was not followed. Today St. Peter's Church, located a block from Ground Zero, the scene of the terrorist attack on the World Trade Center on September 11, 2001, is once again a flourishing residential parish.[27]

With regard to these two powerful dynamics—immigration and neighborhood change—the history of the Church of the Ascension is a microcosm of the history of the archdiocese of New York. Its credentials as part of the immigrant church in New York are incontestable. It was founded to serve the needs of a small local German community, blossomed into a large Irish parish, subsequently became a smaller and predominantly Puerto Rican parish, later evolved into a heavily Dominican parish, and even more recently it has been transformed into a multiethnic and bilingual faith community with a growing middle- and upper-middle-class population.

The people of Ascension parish also suffered their own painful experience of the downward spiral of neighborhood change in the late twentieth century as the quality of life on the Upper West Side deteriorated drastically through three decades of violent crime. However, as resilient New Yorkers, they persevered to witness the Upper West Side recover to become once again one of the most popular residential areas of Manhattan with housing for both those of modest means and a burgeoning upper middle class. Today the Upper West Side is probably more integrated racially and culturally than at any time in the recent past. The Church of the Ascension shares that demographic profile.

The 125th anniversary of the Church of the Ascension is an occasion to celebrate both its past and its present. For more than a century it has served both newly arrived immigrants and parishioners whose roots in America go back many generations. During the past several decades, as the people of Ascension have broadened their understanding of inclusiveness and diversity with the encouragement of Father Duffell and Father Kearney, they have provided a welcoming spiritual home for lesbian, gay, bisexual, and transgender Catholics. As a result, Ascension Catholics can take pride today that they practice their religion by vigorously affirming their Catholic faith at the same time that they assert their quintessential Upper West Side liberal Catholic identity by welcoming to their parish community people of every ethnic background, language, color, sexual orientation, marital status, and social class.

Appendixes

Appendix A: The Pastors of the Church of the Ascension

Father Nicholas M. Reinhart, 1895–1900
Monsignor Edwin M. Sweeny, 1901–23
Bishop Joseph P. Donahue, 1924–59
Monsignor James A. Quinn, 1959–68
Monsignor Richard B. Curtin, 1968–70
Monsignor James J. Wilson, 1970–82
Monsignor John B. Sullivan, Administrator, 1977–81
Father Donald J. Johnston, 1982–94
Father John P. Duffell, 1994–2012
Father Daniel S. Kearney, 2012–present

Appendix B: Upper West Side Catholic Churches in 1865

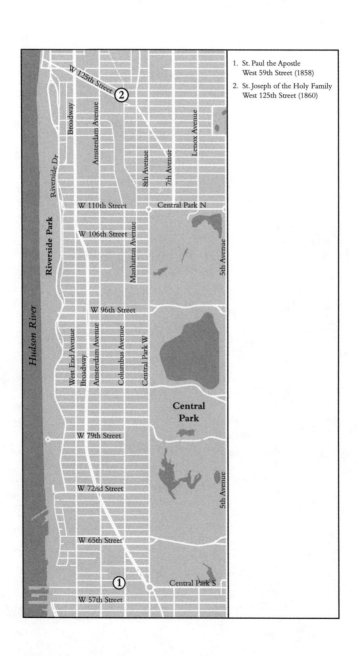

1. St. Paul the Apostle
   West 59th Street (1858)

2. St. Joseph of the Holy Family
   West 125th Street (1860)

Appendix C: Upper West Side Catholic Churches in 1910

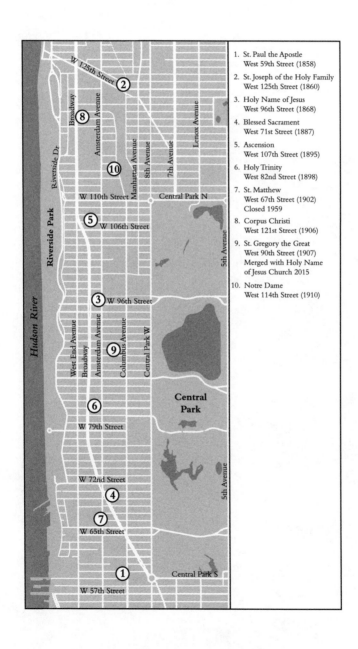

1. St. Paul the Apostle
   West 59th Street (1858)
2. St. Joseph of the Holy Family
   West 125th Street (1860)
3. Holy Name of Jesus
   West 96th Street (1868)
4. Blessed Sacrament
   West 71st Street (1887)
5. Ascension
   West 107th Street (1895)
6. Holy Trinity
   West 82nd Street (1898)
7. St. Matthew
   West 67th Street (1902)
   Closed 1959
8. Corpus Christi
   West 121st Street (1906)
9. St. Gregory the Great
   West 90th Street (1907)
   Merged with Holy Name
   of Jesus Church 2015
10. Notre Dame
    West 114th Street (1910)

Acknowledgments

I wish to thank Father Daniel S. Kearney for inviting me to write a history of the Church of the Ascension to commemorate the 125th anniversary of the parish. It gave me the occasion to deepen my knowledge of the parish and, more important, the opportunity to offer this history to the parishioners of Ascension as an expression of my gratitude to them for their kindness to me during my brief but wonderfully rewarding association with them. I also wish to thank Mrs. Irene Bogoni for her extraordinary generosity in subsidizing the publication of this book. It is only one of her numerous financial benefactions to the Church of the Ascension over the course of many years. Without her generosity, this book would never have seen the light of day.

Two nationally prominent scholars with deep Upper West Side Catholic roots read the entire manuscript and offered me the benefit of their invaluable insights into this unique enclave of the archdiocese of New York. Ms. Margaret O'Brien Steinfels, the former editor of *Commonweal* and a longtime parishioner of Ascension, provided me with numerous personal details of both the decline and renaissance of the parish and the neighborhood. Father Leo J. O'Donovan, S.J., the distinguished Jesuit theologian and President Emeritus of Georgetown University, recalled for me his affectionate childhood recollections of Father George Barry Ford, the dynamic pastor of Corpus Christi Church, and the Dominican Sisters of Sinsinawa, Wisconsin, who staffed Corpus Christi School. They "changed my life forever," he said.

Father John Duffell shared with me his experiences during the transformative eighteen years (1994–2012) that he was pastor of Ascension. My seminary classmate James Welby saved me from many factual errors and offered me his unique insights based on his seven years (1962–69) as an associate pastor of Ascension and his unique perspective before and after his parochial ministry at Ascension as an Upper West Side cradle Catholic. Likewise, Monsignor Robert Stern made available to me his candid unpublished assessment of the Hispanic Apostolate of the Archdiocese of New

York as well as his own experience as an associate pastor of Ascension for three years.

There can be no history without records and no records without archives. In this respect, I am especially grateful to Ms. Kate Feighery, the first professional director of the Archives of the Archdiocese of New York in two centuries (I hope that this factual statement does not make her feel old) and to Cardinal Timothy Michael Dolan, the archbishop of New York and an accomplished church historian in his own right, for appointing Ms. Feighery to this position. I also wish to express my thanks to Ms. Elizabeth Alleva, the former assistant archivist of the archdiocese; Ms. Mindy S. Gordon, the director of archives of the Sisters of Charity of New York; and to Ms. Amy Surak, the archivist of Manhattan College, for giving me access to the archives of the De La Salle Christian Brothers of the former Long Island–New York Province of the Christian Brothers.

I am also grateful to the assistance given to me by Father Anthony Andreassi, C.O.; Sister Regina Baechtle, S.C.; Mr. Michael Elmore; Ms. Robin Brooks Klueber; Mr. Edward McClain; Monsignor Peter O'Donnell; Mr. Preston Smith; and Monsignor John B. Sullivan.

Once again I am deeply indebted to Mr. Fredric Nachbaur, the director of Fordham University Press, for his interest in this book in its initial stages when it was only a proposal and the characteristically meticulous care and the expertise with which he has supervised every aspect of its production. I also owe a great debt to Mr. Eric Newman, the managing editor of Fordham University Press, for his courtesy and support and for the benefit of his superb expertise as a copy editor honed over the past forty-one years. Mr. Mark Lerner, the design and production manager of Fordham University Press, created the strikingly original cover. Mr. Seth Webster, a talented professional photographer and parishioner of Ascension, generously donated the photograph of Ascension Church on the front cover and the two beautiful photographs of the interior of the church.

Last but not least, I wish to thank my sister, Ms. Mary A. Shelley, for her unfailing encouragement and always wise advice.

Thomas J. Shelley,
The Feast of the Ascension
May 30, 2019

Notes

1. A Home of Their Own

1. *New York Times*, June 29, 1896. *New York World*, June 29, 1896.

2. The Bavarian-born William Schickel was also the architect of St. Joseph's Seminary, Dunwoodie, St. Joseph's Church on East 87th Street, and the Church of St. Ignatius Loyola on Park Avenue, his home parish.

3. www.nycago.org/Organs/NYC.img/Ascension.

4. Phyllis Ford, Kathryn D. Horan, and Edmund M. Horan, "A Short History of Ascension Church," *Ascension Church—75th Anniversary*, privately printed.

5. AANY, Minutes of the Meetings of the Diocesan Consultors, December 2, 1896. Earlier that year, the diocesan consultors had warned Reinhart that he would be "swamped" if he incurred more debt. Ibid., February 5, 1896.

2. The Founding Fathers

1. *New York Catholic News*, April 28, 1900. It is estimated that in those years he confirmed 194,000 people.

2. Sulpician Archives of Baltimore, RG 4, Box 36, Corrigan to Charles Rex, S.S., January 30, 1896.

3. John Talbot Smith, *The Catholic Church in New York* (New York: Hall and Locke, 1908), II, 418. Marvin R. O'Connell, *John Ireland and the American Catholic Church* (St. Paul: Minnesota Historical Society Press, 1988), 175. Florence D. Cohalan, *A Popular History of the Archdiocese of New York* (Yonkers: United States Catholic Historical Society, 1983), 108. Robert Emmett Curran, *Michael Augustine Corrigan and the Shaping of Conservative Catholicism in America, 1878–1902* (New York: Arno Press, 1978), vi.

4. *New York Catholic News*, September 23, 1894.

5. Archives of the Archdiocese of New York (hereafter AANY), Minutes of the Meetings of the Diocesan Consultors, October 8, 1890; January 1, February 4, March 4, May 6, 1891; April 5, May 3, December 6, 1893; January 3, June 6, 1894; December 4, 1895.

6. A "national parish" was a parish without territorial boundaries established for the exclusive use of Catholics of a specific ethnic group. Although the Church of the Ascension was established mainly for German-speaking Catholics, it was never a "national parish" in this narrow legalistic definition.

7. The rivalry was due to transatlantic politics. The Church of St. Elizabeth of Hungary supported the authoritarian and chauvinistic Hungarian government that controlled Slovakia. The Church of St. John Nepomucene represented the rising tide of Slovak nationalism.

8. AANY, G-82, Petition of Parishioners of St. Elizabeth of Hungary Church to Archbishop Michael Corrigan, January 8, 1895.

9. Thomas J. Shelley, *Slovaks on the Hudson: Most Holy Trinity Church, Yonkers, and the Slovak Catholics of the Archdiocese of New York, 1894–2000* (Washington: The Catholic University of America Press, 2002), 259. At the Slovak church of St. Mary in Haverstraw, New York, during its early history, there were sixteen pastors in eight years. One of them stayed for six weeks. Ibid., 72.

10. AANY, G-82, Reinhart to Corrigan, April 2, 1895.

11. AANY, Reinhart to Corrigan, Ascension parish file, November 6, 1895.

12. K. Austin Kerr, "Brewing and Distilling," *The Encyclopedia of New York City*, 2nd edn., ed. Kenneth T. Jackson (New Haven and New York: Yale University Press/New-York Historical Society, 2010), 153–154. Both Ehret and his fellow New York beer baron, Peter Doegler, were prominent Catholic laymen and generous benefactors of Catholic institutions, especially Archbishop Corrigan's new seminary at Dunwoodie.

13. *New York World*, January 18, 1896.

14. AANY, Ascension parish file, William R. Ryan to Reinhart, February 3, 1896.

15. Blessed Sacrament Church once owned the corner of West 71st Street and Broadway but sold it for $750,000 to pay for the construction of the church, school, and rectory in the middle of the block. *Golden Jubilee of the Church of the Blessed Sacrament* (New York: Church of the Blessed Sacrament, 1937), 15.

16. AANY, Ascension parish file, Reinhart to Corrigan, November 19, 1895.

17. AANY, Ascension parish file, Reinhart to Corrigan, January 7, 1896.

18. *New York Catholic News*, September 23, 1894.

19. AANY, Ascension parish file, August 13, 1897.

3. The Upper West Side

1. On the history of New Amsterdam, see Russell Shorto, *The Island at the Center of the World: The Epic Story of Dutch Manhattan* (New York: Doubleday, 2004).

2. Edith Wharton, *A Backward Glance* (New York, 1933, reprint New York: Touchstone Edition, 1998), 55.

3. Eric Homberger, *Mrs. Astor's New York: Money and Social Power in a Gilded Age* (New Haven and London: Yale University Press, 2002), xiv, 217. Huntington reneged on the agreement and paid McAllister only $1,000 of the bribe.

4. Edwin G. Burrows and Mike Wallace consider "the Tweed men's fixation on the other side of Central Park" the critical reason for "the sluggish pace of

West Side development." Edwin G. Burrows and Mike Wallace, *Gotham: A History of New York City to 1898* (New York: Oxford University Press, 1999), 929.

5. Alfred Kazin and David Finn, *Our New York* (New York: Harper & Row, 1989), 119.

6. Burrows and Wallace, *Gotham*, 1080. Although Edith Wharton was born in a brownstone on West 23rd Street, she considered brownstone "the most hideous stone ever quarried." Wharton, *A Backward Glance*, 55.

7. *New York Times*, February 22 and March 14, 1880.

8. Henry J. Browne, *One Stop above Hell's Kitchen: Sacred Heart Parish in Clinton* (New York: Church of the Sacred Heart, 1977), 33.

9. Allen J. Share, "Dumbbell Tenements," in *The Encyclopedia of New York City*, ed. Kenneth T. Jackson, 2nd edn. (New York and New Haven: The New-York Historical Society, 2010), 382–83. Richard White, *The Republic for Which It Stands: The United States during Reconstruction and the Gilded Age, 1865–1896* (New York: Oxford University Press, 2017), 512–15.

10. Mike Wallace, *Greater Gotham: A History of New York City from 1898 to 1910* (New York: Oxford University Press, 2017), 5.

11. William Dean Howells, *A Hazard of New Fortunes* (New York: Modern Library Paperback Edition, 2002), 76, 182–83.

12. Charles Lockwood, *Manhattan Moves Uptown: An Illustrated History* (Boston: Houghton Mifflin, 1976), 313–29. I have relied heavily on Lockwood's excellent book for the history of the Upper West Side in the late nineteenth century.

13. Cit. in ibid., 317.

14. Wallace, *Greater Gotham*, 200–94. Schwab's mansion was demolished in 1948 and replaced with an apartment building. In 2018 condominiums were advertised for sale in the renovated Belnord beginning at $3,775,000. *New York Times Magazine*, June 17, 2018.

15. Spann, *The New Metropolis*, 183.

16. Jay P. Dolan, *The Immigrant Church, New York's Irish and German Catholics, 1815–1865* (Baltimore: The Johns Hopkins University Press, 1975), 27–29.

17. Homberger, *Mrs. Astor's New York*, xiv.

18. Sidney Ratner (ed.), *New Light on the History of Great American Fortunes: American Millionaires of 1892 and 1902* (New York: Augustus M. Kelly, Inc., 1953), 57–85. AANY, G-35, Committee on the Celebration of the Episcopal Jubilee of the Most Rev. Michael Augustine Corrigan, May 1898.

19. Burrows and Wallace, *Gotham*, 1095.

20. *New York Times*, January 30 and February 2, 4, 6, 1889. Father McGlynn insisted on being addressed as Dr. McGlynn in recognition of his Roman doctorate.

21. Howells, *A Hazard of New Fortunes*, 402–9. *New York Times*, February 6, 1889.

22. White, *Republic for Which It Stands*, 717.

23. *New York Times*, January 7, 1871.

24. "By all accounts," said Terry Golway, "the title [honest] was not given as an ironic joke." Terry Golway, *Machine Made: Tammany Hall and the Creation of Modern American Politics* (New York: Liveright, 2014), 105.

25. John Talbot Smith, *The Catholic Church in New York* (Boston and New York: Hall and Locke, 1908), II, 446.

26. The other two parishes were Holy Name of Jesus (1868) and Blessed Sacrament (1887).

4. The Ascension Parish Plant

1. Jay P. Dolan, *In Search of an American Catholicism* (New York: Oxford University Press, 2002), 132.

2. Charles Morris, *American Catholic* (New York: Times Books/Random House, 1997), 174.

3. Joseph P. Lyford, *The Airtight Cage: A Study of New York's West Side* (New York: Harper Colophon Books, 1968), 1–6.

4. AANY, Ascension parish file. *New York Times*, obit., November 27, 1923.

5. "Financial Report of the Church of the Ascension from January 1, 1903 to January 1, 1904," *The Calendar: Church of the Ascension*, Vol. III, No. 3 (February 1903): 6–7.

6. *Acta et Decreta Concilii Provincialis Neo-Eboracensis IV* (New York, 1886), 78.

7. AANY, Holy Name parish file, Galligan to Corrigan, September 4, 1894.

8. AANY, Church of Our Lady of Guadalupe, parish file, Zachary Saint-Martin, A.A., to Bishop John J. Dunn, February 28, 1926. Henry Browne, *The Parish of St. Michael, 1857–1957* (New York: The Church of St. Michael, 1957), 26.

9. AANY, C-10, McGlynn to Corrigan, March 11, 1886.

10. *The Calendar: Church of the Ascension*, Vol III, No. 3, 17.

11. AANY, G-2, Mulry to Sirs and Dear Brothers, August 29, 1893. Mulry to Corrigan, November 18, 1893.

12. AANY, G-14, Lowell to Corrigan, November 10, 1897. On Lowell, see Joan Waugh, *Unsentimental Reformer: The Life of Josephine Shaw Lowell* (Cambridge, Mass.: Harvard University Press, 1999).

13. *New York Catholic News*, June 3, 1911.

14. AANY, Ascension parish file, Sweeny to Farley, January 3, 1905. New York *Catholic News*, September 14 and 7, 1912.

15. Sister Marie de Lourdes Walsh, S.C., *The Sisters of Charity of New York, 1809–1959* (New York: Fordham University Press, 1960), II, 104–6. AFSCNY, Brother Eugene O'Gara, F.S.C., The Ascension School, unpaginated.

16. AANY, Ascension parish file, Sweeny to Hayes, June 3, 1916. Sweeny to Farley, May 19, 1916.

17. AANY, Ascension parish file, Sweeny to Farley, May 19, 1916.

18. AANY, Ascension parish file, Sweeny to Hayes, January 29, February 3, 1920.

19. *The Church Bulletin*, February 1923, 9–14.

20. AANY, Ascension parish file, Sweeny to Michael Lavelle, V.G., n.d. [1906].

21. AANY, Holy Name parish file, Delaney to Corrigan, June 3, 1901. Forty years earlier a friendly Protestant visitor at Sunday Mass in St. Stephen's Church on East 28th Street noticed that hardly anyone gave more than a penny in the collection, but every single person gave at least a penny. James Parton, "Our Roman Catholic Brethren," *Atlantic Monthly*, April 28, 1868, 432–35, cit. in Joseph P. Chinnici, O.F.M., and Angelyn Dries, O.F.S., eds., *Prayer and Practice in the American Catholic Community* (Maryknoll, N.Y.: Orbis Books, 2000), 65–68.

22. AANY, Ascension parish file, Sweeny to Lavelle, n.d. [1906].

23. *New York Times*, November 27, 1923.

5. The Confident Years at Ascension

1. The Jesuit Fathers at the Church of St. Francis Xavier on West 16th Street claimed to have heard the astonishing number of 108,728 confessions between August 1862 and August 1873. Archives of the College of St. Francis Xavier, *Litterae Annuae*, Letter of 1862–1863.

2. AANY, parish file, *status animarum* report, 1932.

3. ACA, financial reports, 1928, 1932, 1937. AANY, Ascension parish file, status *animarum* report, 1932.

4. AANY, Ascension parish file, *status animarum* report, 1932.

5. ASCNY, Denis Sheahan, "The West Side Story: Ascension's Class of 1944 holds a Reunion," *House*, November–December 2002, 96–99. There is a copy of the article in the Archives of the Sisters of Charity at Mount St. Vincent, who graciously made it available to me.

6. ASCNY, Graduation Exercises, Class of 1941, Ascension School. ASCNY, Sr. Julia Miriam Schneider, S.C., to Sr. Marie de Lourdes, S.C., n.d.

7. Robert Caro, *Robert Moses and the Fall of New York* (New York: Vintage Books, 1975), 65.

8. Ibid.

9. Ibid., 323. Moses filled Riverside Park with 15 tennis courts, 17 playgrounds, 23 softball fields, 38 basketball courts, 40 handball courts, 13,000 trees, 140,000 feet of footpaths, and 350,000 shrubs.

10. Ibid., 557.

11. Ibid., 561.

6. A Parish in Transition

1. AANY, Ascension parish file, *status animarum* reports 1927, 1932, 1937, 1945, 1949.

2. AANY, Ascension parish file, *status animaum* reports, 1960, 1961.

3. AANY, Ascension parish file, *status animarum* reports, 1971.

4. AFSCNY, Brother Christopher Dardis, F.S.C., to Brother Kenneth Cottrell, F.S.C., Visitation of Ascension School, November 12, 1968. AFSCNY, Brother Christopher Dardis, F.S.C., to Brother Kenneth Cottrell, F.S.C., November 7, 1966.

5. *The Official Catholic Directory* (New York: P. J. Kenedy & Son, 1967), 281, 381; 2017, GS 24.

6. ASCNY, Sister Grace Sabatello, S.C., and Sister Jacqueline Dunne, S.C., to Monsignor James Wilson, April 1, 1974.

7. Gerard O'Hanlon, S.J., "Could a 'Quiet Revolution' Revitalize Irish Catholicism?" *The Tablet*, August 25, 2018.

8. Peter Steinfels, "Contraception and Honesty," *Commonweal*, June 15, 2018. The article originally appeared in *Commonweal*, June 15, 2015.

9. Ana María Díaz-Stevens, *Oxcart Catholicism on Fifth Avenue* (Notre Dame, Ind.: University of Notre Dame Press, 1993), 15.

10. Virginia Sánchez Korrol, "Puerto Ricans," in *Encyclopedia of New York City*, 2nd edn., 1058–60.

11. Virginia Sánchez Korrol, *From Colonia to Community: The History of Puerto Ricans in New York City*, rev. edn. (Berkeley, 1994), 44, cit. in Tyler Anbinder, *City of Dreams* (Boston and New York: Houghton Mifflin Harcourt, 2016), 482.

12. https://en.wikipedia.org/wiki/Puerto_Rican_migration_to_New_York_City.

13. Joseph Berger, "Dominicans Gaining on Puerto Ricans in City," *New York Times*, October 9, 2003.

14. Robert L. Stern, "BIENVENIDOS, BUT . . . The Archdiocese of New York and Ministry to Hispanics, 1952–1982, 12–14." I am deeply grateful to Monsignor Stern for sharing with me this candid unpublished paper. An expurgated version was published by the archdiocese of New York as a chapter in *Hispanics in New York: Religious, Cultural and Social Experiences*; *Hispanos en Nueva York: Experiencias Religiosas, Culturales y Sociales* (New York: Office of Pastoral Research of the Archdiocese of New York, 1982).

15. Joseph P. Fitzpatrick, S.J., Lecture, St. Joseph's Seminary, Dunwoodie, March 3, 1989.

16. The name was quickly changed to the Office of Spanish Community Action and finally to the more inclusive Office of the Spanish-Speaking Apostolate.

17. AANY, Spellman to Cicognani, October 3, 1957. Spellman did not mention the source of this statistic.

18. Díaz-Stevens, *Oxcart Catholicism*, 99.

19. Prior to 1939, the Augustinians of the Assumption administered two Hispanic parishes, Our Lady of Guadalupe on West 14th Street and Our Lady of Esperanza in Washington Heights. The Spanish Vincentians administered La Milagrosa in central Harlem and later Holy Agony in East Harlem. In 1939 Spellman confided St. Cecilia's Church on East 106th Street to the Redemptorists, who had a long record of pastoral experience in Puerto Rico.

20. Stern, "BIENVENIDOS, BUT," 16, 18, 25–27.

21. Díaz-Stevens, *Oxcart Catholicism*, 205.

22. Ibid., 217.

7. *Quo Vadis?*

1. Alan Ehrenhalt, *The Lost City: The Forgotten Virtues of Community in America* (Basic Books, 1995), 120.

2. AANY, Ascension parish file, Concerned Parishioners of Ascension to Archbishop Cooke, July 19, 1968, unpublished paper. I am grateful to James Welby, my seminary classmate, for explaining to me the origins and evolution of the search committee.

3. Manhattan Avenue is one of the borough's shortest and least-known north–south thoroughfares. It extends from West 100th Street to West 124th Street between Columbus Avenue/Morningside Park and Central Park West/Frederick Douglass Boulevard.

4. AANY, Ascension parish file, Concerned Parishioners of Ascension to Archbishop Cooke, July 19, 1968.

5. On the Church of St. Benedict the Moor, see Jack M. Arlotta, "Before Harlem: Black Catholics in the Archdiocese of New York and the Church of St. Benedict the Moor," *Dunwoodie Review* 16 (1992–1993): 69–108.

6. AANY, A-52, Bishop John McGill to Archbishop John McCloskey, June 14, 1869.

7. *New York Sun*, January 21, 1871.

8. Thomas J. Shelley, "A Good Man but Crazy on Some Points: Father Thomas Farrell and Liberal Catholicism in Nineteenth-Century New York," *Revue d'Histoire Ecclésiastique* 97:1 (2002): 110–32. See also Robert Emmett Curran, "'Prelude to Americanism': The New York Accademia and Clerical Radicalism in the Late Nineteenth Century," *Church History* 47 (1978): 48–65.

9. Archives of the Diocese of Rochester, Corrigan to McQuaid, December 28, 1892.

10. Robert Emmett Curran, *Michael Augustine Corrigan and the Shaping of Conservative Catholicism in America, 1878–1902* (New York: Arno Press, 1978), 241. Florence D. Cohalan, *A Popular History of the Archdiocese of New York* (Yonkers: United States Catholic Historical Society, 1983), 136.

11. *New York Times*, November 30, 1980, obit of Browne. I am grateful to Ms. Margaret O'Brien Steinfels for bringing this obit to my attention.

12. Cit. in Joseph P. Lyford, *The Airtight Cage: A Study of New York's West Side* (New York: Harper Colophon Books, 1968), 125.

13. AANY, parish file of St. Gregory the Great. Henry J. Browne, *Groping for Relevance in an Urban Parish: St. Gregory the Great, N.Y.C., 1968–1970*, 5–7. Unpublished paper.

14. Kenneth A. Briggs, "A Calm Voice in an Age of Upheaval," *New York Times*, October 7, 1983.

15. *Ascension Church Bulletin*, March 1970.

16. Robert L. Stern, "BIENVENIDOS, BUT . . . The Archdiocese of New York and Ministry to Hispanics, 1952–1982," 24, 32.

17. AANY, Holy Name parish file, Patrick V. McNamara to Lawrence J. Kenney, November 10, 1972.

18. Once again, I am grateful to James Welby for clarifying this aspect of Ascension history for me.

19. AANY, Ascension parish file, *El Comité de Cristianos pro Justicia* to Estimado Monseñor, October 9, 1971. Wilson to *El Comité*, n.d.

20. AANY, Ascension parish file, Wilson, Acerca del Traslado del Padre Pedro, n.d.

21. AANY, Ascension parish file, Wilson to Mahoney, October 17, 1971.

22. Cit. in Edward Norman, *The English Catholic Church in the Nineteenth Century* (Oxford: Clarendon Press, 1984), 4.

23. AANY, Ascension parish file, Head to Wilson, October 24, 1972.

24. *Ascension Church Bulletin*, March 1970, December 1972. One reason for the large debt in 1969 was the expenditure of $48,770.36 on repairs in and renovations to the school.

25. Calvin Trillin, "Democracy in Action (1988)," in *Making the Irish American, History and Heritage of the Irish in the United States*, eds. J. J Lee and Marion R. Casey (New York: Glucksman Ireland House and New York University Press, 2007), 535.

26. James Flanagan, "The Land That Columbus Loved Best," *Ascension Church Bulletin*, April 1972, 16–18.

27. John T. Ridge, "New York's Irish Seaside Resorts," *New York Irish History* 31(2017): 55–56.

28. AANY, St. Gregory parish file, Henry J. Browne, *Groping for Relevance in an Urban Parish*, unpublished paper, [1970–?].

8. A Neighborhood in Peril

1. Alfred Kazin, "The Upper West Side," *New York Times*, March 12, 1978. Kazin grew up in Brownsville, when, he said, it was a "promising American ghetto" known as "Brunzvil."

2. Joseph P. Lyford, *The Airtight Cage: A Study of New York's West Side* (New York: Harper Colophon Books, 1968), 24–25.

3. Ibid., xx–xxi.

4. Joseph P. Fried, "Living on the West Side: A Study of Wide Diversity," *New York Times*, May 25, 1969.

5. Lyford, *Airtight Cage*, 301.

6. Ibid., 320.

7. AANY, Browne, St. Gregory's Parish File, *Groping for Relevance*, 21–23.

8. Flavia Alaya, *Under the Rose* (New York: The Feminist Press, 1999). See also Margaret O'Brien Steinfels, "Everybody called him 'Father,'" *Commonweal*, January 14, 2000.

9. Lyford, *Airtight Cage*, 318.

10. John Podhoretz, "The Upper West Side, Then and Now," *Commentary*, May 2010, 27–31.

11. Neither Podhoretz nor Robert Caro specifies how many of the original tenants were evicted to make way for Manhattan Inc., but Caro estimated that, between 1945 and 1952, 170,000 residents were evicted throughout New York City as a result of Moses's public works projects. Robert Caro, *Robert Moses and the Fall of New York* (New York: Vintage Books, 1975), 964, 967, 970–71, 1010–12.

12. *New York Times*, December 1, 2013. Podhoretz, "Upper West Side," 31.

13. John Rousmaniere, "Upper West Side," *Encyclopedia of New York City*, 2nd edn., 1353. Lyford, *Glass Cage*, 277.

14. Lyford, *Glass Cage*, 276.

15. Jeffrey Goldberg, "The Decline and Fall of the Upper West Side, *New York Magazine*, April 24, 1994, 37–42.

16. Adam Gopnik, "After the Fall," *The New Yorker*, February 12 & 19, 2018, 93.

17. ASCNY, Your Sisters at Ascension to Dear Sisters, October 1963.

9. Recovery and Renaissance

1. AANY, Ascension parish file, *status animarum* Report, 1961, 1972, 1982, 1991, 1994.

2. AANY, Mary Sanz to Msgr. Thomas Leonard, October 8, 1976. Father Sullivan remained administrator of Ascension until 1981.

3. Fox Butterfield, "Upper West Side's '2 Worst Drug Blocks,'" *New York Times*, June 18, 1988.

4. Margaret O'Brien Steinfels was an eyewitness to this grotesque practice. The Straus Memorial contains the inspiring but heartbreaking quotation from 2 Samuel 1:23, "Lovely and pleasant were they in their lives and in their death they were not parted."

5. www 1, nyc.gov./site/nypd/ComptStat/24th precinct/vol. 24/number 26.

6. Adam Gopnik, "After the Fall," *The New Yorker*, February 12 & 19, 2018.

7. Tyler Anbinder, *City of Dreams* (Boston and New York: Houghton Mifflin Harcourt, 2016), 513–20. For this treatment of the Dominicans in New York City, I have relied heavily on Anbinder's excellent account.

8. Ibid., 521.

9. Center for Latin American, Caribbean and Latino Studies at CUNY Graduate Center, cit. in *New York Post*, November 13, 2014.

10. ACA, Evaluation of Ascension Church, n.d.

11. Father John Duffell to author, May 18, 2018.

12. Mary Ann Poust, "The Big A," *Catholic New York*, February 1, 1996.

13. Father John Duffell to author, February 17, 2018.

14. John Sullivan, "From a Manhattan Congregation, a 'Flood of Food' to Help the Hungry," *New York Times*, November 29, 1996.

15. Professor Franklin Zimring of the University of California, cit. in George L. Kelling, "How New York Became Safe: The Full Story," *City Journal*, special issue, 2009.

16. Matt Ford, "What Caused the Great Crime Decline in the U.S.?" *The Atlantic*, April 15, 2016.

17. Patrick Sharkey, *Uneasy Peace: The Great Crime Decline, the Renewal of City Life, and the Next War on Violence* (New York and London: W. W. Norton & Company, 2018), 60, 30.

18. James Panero, "The Unending Battle for the Upper West Side," *City Journal*, summer 2012. Ms. Margaret O'Brien Steinfels first called my attention to the significance of what James Panero described as "the cooperative revolution."

19. www.l,nyc.gov/site/nypd/CompStat/24thprecinct/vol,24/number 26. Sharkey, *Uneasy Peace*, 98, 10.

20. David W. Dunlap, "A Neighborhood Wavers in Its Liberal Tradition," *New York Times*, November 3, 1989.

21. AANY, St. Gregory parish file, Henry J. Browne, *Groping for Relevance in an Urban Parish*, unpublished paper, [1970–?].

22. Jennifer Medina, "Changing with Times, a Parish Prospers," *New York Times*, April 6, 2008.

23. Thomas J. Shelley, *Greenwich Village Catholics: St. Joseph's Church and the Evolution of an Urban Faith Community* (Washington: The Catholic University of America Press, 2003), 255.

24. Archives of St. Joseph's Church, Greenwich Village, Tos to Sheridan et al., May 16, 1994. Tos to O'Connor, July 21, 1997.

10. Old and New Horizons

1. AANY, Ascension Parish File, *status animarum* Report, 1982. ACA, *status animarum* Report, 2013.

2. Father John Duffell to author, May 18, 2018.

3. ACA, *status animarum* Report, 2017.

4. Lawrence Kehoe (ed.), *Complete Works of the Most Rev. John Hughes* (New York: Lawrence Kehoe, 1866), II, 715.

5. Ms. Robin Brooks Klueber to author, June 19, 2018.

6. *Ascension Parish Bulletin*, January 21, 2018. ACA, *status animarum* Report, 2017.

7. *Ascension Parish Bulletin*, September 30, 2017. ACA, GAAP Compliant Statement of Activities, August 2017.

8. AANY, Corpus Christi parish file, McIntyre to Ford, August 6, 1938. McIntyre to Ford, February 11, 1941. When Archbishop Paul Hallinan of Atlanta first met Cardinal McIntyre at Vatican II, he summed up his impression of him in two words: "absolutely stupid." Archives of the Diocese of Cleveland, Hallinan, diary, October 16, 1962.

9. AANY, Corpus Christi parish file, Ford to Gaffney, October 11, 1951.

10. AANY, Corpus Christi file, Ford to Maguire, March 1, 1954. Ford described his contribution to Corpus Christi and to the Catholic Church in Morningside Heights in his autobiography, *A Degree of Difference* (New York: Farrar, Straus & Giroux, 1969). See also E. Harold Smith, *The History of Corpus Christi Parish, 1906–1956* (New York: Corpus Christi Church, 1956).

11. AANY, Corpus Christi parish file, Ford to Hayes, June 12, 1935.

12. Father Raymond M. Rafferty to author, November 11, 2018.

13. Father Leo J. O'Donovan, S.J., to author, November 21, 2018.

14. J. M. Cameron, "Dorothy Day (1897–1980)," *New York Review of Books*, January 22, 1981.

15. Retention Center, St. Joseph's Seminary, Dunwoodie, McIntyre to Cicognani, April 22, 1936.

16. Kate Hennessy, *Dorothy Day, The World Will Be Saved by Beauty* (New York: Scribner's, 2017), 133–34.

17. Retention Center, St. Joseph's Seminary, Dunwoodie, O'Connor to McIntyre, February 9, 1942. For a fuller treatment of the relationship between Dorothy Day and Cardinal McIntyre, see Thomas A. Lynch, "Dorothy Day & Cardinal McIntyre: Not Poles Apart," *Church* 10 (Summer 1992): 10–15.

18. Francis P. Duffy, "Does Theology Preserve Religion?" *American Ecclesiastical Review* 25 (1901): 372–90. Pope John XXIII said on October 11, 1962, "The substance of the ancient doctrine of the faith is one thing, and the way in which it is presented is another." Giuseppe Alberigo and Joseph A. Komonchak (eds.), *History of Vatican II* (Maryknoll, N.Y., and Leuven: Orbis Books, 1997), II, 17.

19. Duffy, ibid. AANY, I–16, Farley to Archbishop Pellegrino F. Stagni, O.S.M., March 4, 1913. "Modernism" was condemned by Pope Pius X in the encyclical *Pascendi dominici gregis* in September 1907. The learned and witty French church historian Monsignor Louis Duchesne, who shared many of Duffy's views, said that the encyclical should have been called *Digitus in Oculo*, "Finger in the Eye." Adrien Dansette, *Histoire Religieuse de la France Contemporaine* (Paris: Flammarion, 1951), II, 443.

20. *New York Times*, February 26, March 7, 1921.

21. "Catholic and Patriot: Governor Smith Replies," *Atlantic Monthly*, 139 (May 1927): 721–28. Thomas J. Shelley, "'What the Hell Is an Encyclical?' Governor Alfred E. Smith, Charles C. Marshall, Esq., and Father Francis P. Duffy," *U.S. Catholic Historian* 15:2 (1999): 23–49.

22. Library of Congress, Manuscript Division, Charles C. Marshall Papers, Duffy to Frederic R. Coudert, June 3, 1927.

23. AANY, Q-17, Bonzano to Hayes, July 4, 1927.

24. Alexander Woollcott, *While Rome Burns* (New York: The Viking Press, 1934), 49–50. On Duffy, see Thomas J. Shelley, "Father Francis Patrick Duffy, a Very Irish, Very Catholic, Very American Person," *Breifne: Journal of Cumann Seanchaise Bhreifne (Breifne Historical Society)* X (2004): 176–95.

25. It is the title of Dolan's classic study of antebellum New York Catholicism, *The Immigrant Church: New York's Irish and German Catholics, 1815–1865* (Baltimore: The Johns Hopkins University Press, 1975).

26. Norbert H. Miller, O.F.M. Cap., "Pioneer Catholic Missionaries in the United States, 1784–1816," *Historical Records and Studies* 21 (1932): 182, 185.

27. AANY, Minutes of the Meetings of the Board of Diocesan Consultors, December 2, 1896, December 7, 1898.

Bibliography

Archival Sources

Archives of the Archdiocese of New York
Archives of the Church of the Ascension
Archives of the College of St. Francis Xavier, New York City
Archives of the De La Salle Brothers of the Christian Schools
Archives of the Diocese of Cleveland
Archives of the Diocese of Rochester
Archives of the Sisters of Charity of New York
Archives of St. Joseph's Church, Greenwich Village, New York City
The Ascension Church Bulletin
The Calendar: Church of the Ascension
Library of Congress, Manuscript Division, Charles C. Marshall Papers
Retention Center, St. Joseph's Seminary, Dunwoodie, Yonkers, New York
Sulpician Archives of Baltimore

Books

Acta et Decreta Concilii Provincialis Neo-Eboracensis IV. New York, 1886.
Alaya, Flavia. *Under the Rose*. New York: The Feminist Press, 1999.
Alberigo, Giuseppe, and Joseph A. Komonchak, eds. *History of Vatican II*. 5 vols. Maryknoll, N.Y., and Leuven: Orbis Books 1997.
Anbinder, Tyler. *City of Dreams*. Boston and New York: Houghton Mifflin Harcourt, 2016.
Browne, Henry J. *One Stop above Hell's Kitchen: Sacred Heart Parish in Clinton*. New York: Church of the Sacred Heart, 1977.
———. *The Parish of St. Michael, 1857–1957*. New York: The Church of St. Michael, 1957.
Burrows, Edwin G., and Mike Wallace. *Gotham: A History of New York City to 1898*. New York: Oxford University Press, 1999.
Caro, Robert. *Robert Moses and the Fall of New York*. New York: Vintage Books, 1975.
Chinnici, Joseph P., O.F.M., and Angelyn Dries, O.S.F., eds. *Prayer and Practice in the American Catholic Community*. Maryknoll: Orbis Books, 2000.

Cohalan, Florence D. *A Popular History of the Archdiocese of New York.* Yonkers, N.Y.: U.S. Historical Society, 1983.

Curran, Robert Emmett. *Michael Augustine Corrigan and the Shaping of Conservative Catholicism in America, 1878–1902.* New York: Arno Press, 1978.

Dansette, Adrien. *Histoire religeuse de la France Contemporaine.* 2 vols. Paris: Flammarion, 1951.

Díaz-Stevens, Ana María. *Oxcart Catholicism on Fifth Avenue.* Notre Dame, Ind.: University of Notre Dame Press, 1993.

Dolan, Jay P. *The Immigrant Church: New York's Irish and German Catholics, 1815–1865.* Baltimore: The Johns Hopkins University Press, 1975.

———. *In Search of an American Catholicism.* New York: Oxford University Press, 2002.

Ehrenhalt, Alan. *The Lost City: The Forgotten Virtues of Community in America.* New York: Basic Books, 1995.

Ford, George Barry. *A Degree of Difference.* New York: Farrar, Straus & Giroux, 1969.

Golden Jubilee of the Church of the Blessed Sacrament. New York: Church of the Blessed Sacrament, 1937.

Golway, Terry. *Machine Made: Tammany Hall and the Creation of Modern American Politics.* New York: Liveright, 2014.

Hennessy, Kate. *Dorothy Day: The World Will Be Saved by Beauty.* New York: Scribner's, 2017.

Homberger, Eric. *Mrs. Astor's New York: Money and Social Power in a Gilded Age.* New Haven and London: Yale University Press, 2002.

Howells, William Dean. *A Hazard of New Fortunes.* New York: Modern Library Paperback Edition, 2002.

Jackson, Kenneth T., ed. *Encyclopedia of the City of New York.* Second Edition. New Haven and New York: Yale University Press and the New-York Historical Society, 2010.

Kazin, Alfred, and David Finn. *Our New York.* New York: Harper & Row, 1989.

Kehoe, Lawrence, ed. *Complete Works of the Most Reverend John Hughes.* 2 vols. New York: Lawrence Kehoe, 1866.

Lee, J. J., and Marion R. Casey, eds. *Making the Irish American: History and Heritage of the Irish in America.* New York: Glucksman Ireland House and New York University Press, 2007.

Lockwood, Charles. *Manhattan Moves Uptown: An Illustrated History.* Boston: Houghton Mifflin Company, 1976.

Lyford, Joseph P. *The Airtight Cage: A Study of New York's West Side.* New York: Harper Colophon Books, 1968.

Morris, Charles. *American Catholic.* New York: Times Books/Random House, 1997.

Norman, Edward. *The English Catholic Church in the Nineteenth Century.* Oxford: Clarendon Press, 1984.

O'Connell, Marvin R. *John Ireland and the American Catholic Church.* St. Paul: Minnesota Historical Society, 1988.

Ratner, Sidney, ed. *New Light on the History of the Great American Fortunes: American Millionaires of 1892 and 1902.* New York: Augustus M. Kelly, Inc., 1953.

Sharkey, Patrick. *Uneasy Peace: The Great Crime Decline, the Renewal of City Life, and the Next War on Violence.* New York and London: W. W. Norton & Company, 2018.

Shelley, Thomas J. *Greenwich Village Catholics: St. Joseph's Church and the Evolution of an Urban Faith Community, 1829–2002.* Washington: The Catholic University of America Press, 2003.

———. *Slovaks on the Hudson: Most Holy Trinity Church, Yonkers, and the Slovaks of the Archdiocese of New York, 1894–2002.* Washington: The Catholic University of America Press, 2002.

Shorto, Russell. *The Island at the Center of the World: The Epic Story of Dutch Manhattan.* New York: Doubleday, 2004.

Smith, E. Harold. *The History of Corpus Christi Parish, 1906–1956.* New York: Corpus Christi Church, 1956.

Smith, John Talbot. *The Catholic Church in New York.* 2 vols. Boston and New York: Hall and Locke, 1904.

Spann, Edward K. *The New Metropolis: New York City, 1840–1857.* New York: Columbia University Press, 1981.

Wallace, Mike. *Greater Gotham: A History of New York from 1898 to 1919.* New York: Oxford University Press, 2017.

Walsh, Sister Marie de Lourdes. *The Sisters of Charity of New York, 1809–1959.* 3 vols. New York: Fordham University Press, 1960.

Waugh, Joan. *Unsentimental Reformer: The Life of Josephine Shaw Lowell.* Cambridge, Mass.: Harvard University Press, 1999.

Wharton, Edith. *A Backward Glance.* New York, 1933, reprint New York: Touchstone Edition, 1998.

White, Richard. *The Republic for Which It Stands: The United States during Reconstruction and the Gilded Age, 1865–1896.* New York: Oxford University Press, 2017.

Woollcott, Alexander. *While Rome Burns.* New York: The Viking Press, 1934.

Articles

Arlotta, Jack M. "Before Harlem: Black Catholics in the Archdiocese of New York and the Church of St. Benedict the Moor." *Dunwoodie Review* 16 (1992–93): 69–108.

"Catholic and Patriot: Governor Smith Replies." *Atlantic Monthly* 139 (May 1927): 721–28.

Curran, Robert Emmett. "Prelude to 'Americanism': The New York Accademia and Clerical Radicalism in the Late Nineteenth Century." *Church History* 47 (1978): 48–65.

Duffy, Francis P. "Does Theology Preserve Religion?" *American Ecclesiastical Review*, 25 (1901): 372–90.

Ford, Matt. "What Caused the Great Crime Decline in the U.S.?" *The Atlantic*, April 15, 2016.

Ford, Phyllis, Kathryn Moran, and Edmund Horan. "A Short History of Ascension Church." *Ascension Church–75th Anniversary*, privately printed.

Goldberg, Jeffrey. "The Decline and Fall of the Upper West Side." *New York*, April 24, 1994, 37–42.

Gopnik, Adam. "After the Fall." *The New Yorker*, February 12 & 19, 2018.

Kelling, George L. "How New York Became Safe: The Full Story." *City Journal*, special issue, 2009.

Lynch, Thomas A. "Dorothy Day and Cardinal McIntyre: Not Poles Apart." *Church* 8 (Summer 1992): 10–15.

Miller, Norbert H., O.F.M. Cap. "Pioneer Catholic Missionaries in the United States, 1784–1816." *Historical Records and Studies* 21 (1932): 182–85.

Panero, James. "The Unending Battle for the Upper West Side." *City Journal*, summer 2012.

Podhoretz, John. "The Upper West Side, Then and Now." *Commentary*, May 2010, 27–31.

Ridge, John T. "New York's Irish Seaside Resorts." *New York Irish History* 31(2017): 49–62.

Shelley, Thomas J. "Father Francis Patrick Duffy: A Very Irish, Very Catholic, Very American Person." *Breifne: Journal of Cumann Seanchais Bhreifne (Breifne Historical Society)* X (2004): 176–95.

———. "A Good Man but Crazy on Some Points: Father Thomas Farrell and Liberal Catholicism in Nineteenth-Century New York." *Revue d'Histoire Ecclésiastique* 97:1 (2002): 110–32.

———. "'What the Hell Is an Encyclical?' Governor Alfred E. Smith, Charles C. Marshall, Esq., and Father Francis P. Duffy." *U.S. Catholic Historian*, 15:2 (1999): 23–49.

Steinfels, Margaret O'Brien. "Everybody called him 'Father.'" *Commonweal*, January 14, 2000.

Steinfels, Peter. "Contraception and Honesty." *Commonweal*, June 15, 2018.

Newspapers

Catholic New York
New York Catholic News
New York Post
New York Review of Books
New York Sun
New York Times
New York Times Magazine
New York World
The Catholic Worker
The Tablet

Unpublished Papers

Browne, Henry J. *Groping for Relevance in an Urban Parish: St. Gregory the Great.* New York City, 1968–1970.

Concerned Parishioners [of Ascension Parish] to Most Reverend Terence J. Cooke. July 19, 1968.

Stern, Robert L. *BIENVENIDOS BUT . . . The Archdiocese of New York and Ministry to Hispanics, 1952–1982.*

Index

Monsignor Thomas J. Shelley, a priest of the archdiocese of New York, is Emeritus Professor of Church History at Fordham University. His publications include *Bicentennial History of the Archdiocese of New York* (Strasbourg, 2008) and *Fordham, A History of the Jesuit University of New York: 1841–2003* (Fordham, 2016).

Select titles from Empire State Editions

ESE

Salvatore Basile, *Fifth Avenue Famous: The Extraordinary Story of Music at St. Patrick's Cathedral*. Foreword by Most Reverend Timothy M. Dolan, Archbishop of New York

Andrew J. Sparberg, *From a Nickel to a Token: The Journey from Board of Transportation to MTA*

New York's Golden Age of Bridges. Paintings by Antonio Masi, Essays by Joan Marans Dim, Foreword by Harold Holzer

Daniel Campo, *The Accidental Playground: Brooklyn Waterfront Narratives of the Undesigned and Unplanned*

Gerard R. Wolfe, *The Synagogues of New York's Lower East Side: A Retrospective and Contemporary View, Second Edition*. Photographs by Jo Renée Fine and Norman Borden, Foreword by Joseph Berger

Joseph B. Raskin, *The Routes Not Taken: A Trip Through New York City's Unbuilt Subway System*

Tom Glynn, *Reading Publics: New York City's Public Libraries, 1754–1911*

R. Scott Hanson, *City of Gods: Religious Freedom, Immigration, and Pluralism in Flushing, Queens*. Foreword by Martin E. Marty

Dorothy Day and the Catholic Worker: The Miracle of Our Continuance. Edited, with an Introduction and Additional Text by Kate Hennessy, Photographs by Vivian Cherry, Text by Dorothy Day

Robert Weldon Whalen, *Murder, Inc., and the Moral Life: Gangsters and Gangbusters in La Guardia's New York*

Sharon Egretta Sutton, *When Ivory Towers Were Black: A Story about Race in America's Cities and Universities*

Pamela Hanlon, *A Wordly Affair: New York, the United Nations, and the Story Behind Their Unlikely Bond*

Britt Haas, *Fighting Authoritarianism: American Youth Activism in the 1930s*

David J. Goodwin, *Left Bank of the Hudson: Jersey City and the Artists of 111 1st Street*. Foreword by DW Gibson

Nandini Bagchee, *Counter Institution: Activist Estates of the Lower East Side*

Susan Celia Greenfield (ed.), *Sacred Shelter: Thirteen Journeys of Homelessness and Healing*

Elizabeth Macaulay Lewis and Matthew M. McGowan (eds.), *Classical New York: Discovering Greece and Rome in Gotham*

Colin Davey with Thomas A. Lesser, *The American Museum of Natural History and How It Got That Way*. Foreword by Kermit Roosevelt III

Lolita Buckner Inniss, *The Princeton Fugitive Slave: The Trials of James Collins Johnson*

Wendy Jean Katz, *Humbug: The Politics of Art Criticism in New York City's Penny Press*

Lady Liberty: An Illustrated History of America's Most Storied Woman. Essays by Joan Marans Dim, paintings by Antonio Masi

For a complete list, visit www.fordhampress.com/empire-state-editions.